"Many leaders struggle to lead disruptive change. *Leading Transformation* provides new tools to overcome the old hurdles to success."

—**CLAYTON M. CHRISTENSEN**, Kim B. Clark Professor of Business Administration, Harvard Business School; bestselling author, *The Innovator's Dilemma*

"*Leading Transformation* is the most original and thought-provoking book I've ever read on how to design and inspire organizational change. The authors show how using proven tools from places I never expected—science fiction, comics, and rap music, for example—can fuel remarkable cultural and technological transformations. This is the rare business book that is fun to read, will make you think differently about leadership, and teach you new skills."

—**ROBERT SUTTON**, Professor of Management Science and Engineering, Stanford University; bestselling author, *Good Boss, Bad Boss* and *Scaling Up Excellence*

"In my first days as CEO of ING I was given some sound advice: think of yourself rather as the CSO, the Chief Storytelling Officer. Nathan Furr and his coauthors perfectly explain why this is true. Transformation starts with a visionary and compelling story. A story built on an aspirational purpose. A story that wins hearts and minds."

—**RALPH HAMERS**, CEO, ING Group

"Packed with inspirational stories, counterintuitive approaches, and practical tools, *Leading Transformation* is an absolute must-read for executives facing disruptive change. Science fiction, cartoons, neuroprototypes, and artifact trails are sure to become standard components of the strategist's toolkit."

—**SCOTT D. ANTHONY**, Senior Partner, Innosight; author, *Dual Transformation* and *The Little Black Book of Innovation*

"Identifying breakthrough technologies that pose a threat or opportunity is one thing—having the methodology, the courage, and the endurance to lead a transformation to deal with them is wholly another. Kyle Nel's work at Lowe's and the many examples of how to leverage behavioral economics and applied neuroscience make this book one of the most important guides for navigating the accelerating changes affecting businesses today."

—ROB NAIL, CEO and Associate Founder, Singularity University

"*Leading Transformation* gives business leaders new and practical tools required to make real behavioral change."

—MARC GOODMAN, *New York Times*–bestselling author, *Future Crimes*

"A provocative and compelling book that synthesizes the scientific research and experiential insight so well, it convinced me that the secret to behavior change often starts with counterintuitive storytelling—both for ourselves and when leading others."

—PETER SIMS, founder and CEO, Parliament, Inc.; author, *Little Bets*

"There has never been a more important time for organizations to prepare for the future and embrace an abundance mindset, and this book is an indispensable guide for how to do it. It's full of sci-fi inspiration and real-world examples to lead those of us who believe that our organizations can transform to create lasting change by changing behavior—both within our organizations and within ourselves."

—PETER DIAMANDIS, founder and Chairman, XPRIZE Foundation; cofounder and Executive Chairman, Singularity University

LEADING TRANSFORMATION

LEADING TRANSFORMATION

How to Take Charge of Your Company's Future

Nathan Furr, Kyle Nel,
and Thomas Zoëga Ramsøy

HARVARD BUSINESS REVIEW PRESS

Boston, Massachusetts

Library of Congress Cataloging-in-Publication Data

Names: Furr, Nathan R., author. | Nel, Kyle, author. | Ramsøy, Thomas Zoëga, author.
Title: Leading transformation : how to take charge of your company's future / Nathan Furr, Kyle Nel, and Thomas Zoëga Ramsøy.
Description: Boston, Massachusetts : Harvard Business Review Press, [2018] | Includes index.
Identifiers: LCCN 2018017713 | ISBN 9781633696549 (hardcover : alk. paper)
Subjects: LCSH: Industrial management. | Leadership. | Technological innovations.
Classification: LCC HD31.2 .F87 2018 | DDC 658.4/063—dc23
LC record available at https://lccn.loc.gov/2018017713

The paper used in this publication meets the requirements of the American National Standard for Permanence of Paper for Publications and Documents in Libraries and Archives Z39.48-1992.

ISBN: 9781633696549
eISBN: 9781633696556

CONTENTS

LEADING
TRANSFORMATION

ONE

How Companies Transform

In 2012, Lowe's, the North American hardware retailer, was in a familiar spot. Despite being one of the leading home improvement retailers (selling hammers, paint, and other products to the $30 billion North American DIY and professional market), Lowe's never seemed able to catch up to archrival The Home Depot, let alone be first in its industry. To make matters worse, a quick glance at a retail outlet map revealed an overwhelming sea of stores saturating the market. Searching for growth, Lowe's had begun expansion forays into Canada, Mexico, and Australia. But results had been disappointing; an acquisition attempt had been publicly thwarted in Canada, while store closings and corporate layoffs were taking place in the United States.[1] Meanwhile, several promising innovation efforts had fallen flat, leading to more losses and unfulfilled growth promises. As Lowe's faced its future under the harsh spotlight of quarterly earnings pressure, the retailer seemed caught in the same bind that troubles so many other large companies: the company was big, profitable, risk-averse, and tethered by quarterly earnings. Its own success in retail meant that it lacked the motivation, capabilities, or support from shareholders to do something transformational. The future looked like more of the same; Lowe's expected a grinding battle to try to break out of second place.

Fast-forward six years to 2018. Lowe's has helped send the first 3-D printer into outer space, developed the first 3-D print and scan services in stores, and built some of the first 3-D imaging capabilities in the world.[2] It has also introduced some of the first retail robots in actual use; they greet customers in stores and take inventory at night.[3] Lowe's is also developing exosuits—external robotic skeletons that help workers carry heavy items.[4] Even more surprising, it sold augmented-reality (AR) phones through a collaboration with Google and Lenovo.[5] More importantly, these imaginative initiatives are succeeding. The phone flew off shelves, and the 3-D imaging capabilities have been shown to increase conversion of online sales for some items by more than 50 percent.[6] The robots are addressing the expensive challenge of keeping accurate inventory when you have a hundred thousand-plus in-store products. The exosuits have generated interest from around the world.[7]

In addition, Lowe's reputation for innovation has risen dramatically. The company became an unlikely number one in retail innovation on the *Fortune* World's Most Admired Companies list and number one for AR or virtual reality (VR) on *Fast Company*'s Most Innovative Companies list, even higher than the company that makes the leading 3-D development platform! Meanwhile, since 2012, the stock price increased nearly threefold, adding $45 billion in market capitalization to the company. But what's more important than all these measures, Lowe's itself has begun to change—from an ossified giant in the past to an agile, adaptable company taking charge of its future. By any measure, something transformational happened.

Who We Are, and Why We Wrote This Book

Transformation may be one of the hardest things leaders are called on to do. By transformation, we mean seeing the possible, valuable futures for your organization and then successfully overcoming the barriers to creating that future. An organization undergoing transformation might lead a disruptive new business model, a radical innovation, a strategy reorientation, a cultural makeover, or some other significant change. But transformation always requires you to dream bigger about what else your organization can do and then to do something meaningful about it.

Leaders know that their job is to lead transformation to keep pace with technology and an ever-changing business environment. They also know that they are bound to fail doing so. But this discouraging outcome is not because they can't solve a technological or strategic problem. Leaders will fail because of intractable human problems associated with change—problems such as fear, habits, politics, and lack of imagination. These challenges have always plagued humans, but what if we had a way to transcend them?

This book reveals a radical new method for doing just that—for driving the kind of change described above at Lowe's and for addressing the real, human challenges of change. As an author team, we bring a unique perspective to this topic. Written by the executive who designed and implemented the process we describe in this book (Kyle), the neuroscientist who designed measurement tools for applying this process to unfamiliar territories (Thomas), and the academic who explains why and how the process works (Nathan), the book introduces an innovative yet proven way of creating breakthrough change. Demonstrated at Lowe's and Walmart—large organizations that are slow to change—the transformation process and tools have also been used successfully by organizations such as IKEA, Pepsi, Google, Microsoft, XPRIZE, the United Nations, and many others we cannot name. Most importantly, the transformation process has been applied not just by the Googles of the world, but by everyday companies, governments, and nongovernmental organizations (NGOs) to create real change.

Our goal with this book is to describe the transformation process and tools that worked for us and for leaders at many organizations around the world. Rather than describe what we have done

individually, much of the time we used the term *we* to emphasize this shared journey to communicate to you the tools to create
an inspiring vision and then to make it happen. We hope to provide you with a road map for leading transformation in your company. Although we can't cover everything about transformation in
a single book, and we each came from different starting points—
manager, scientist, professor—all of us sought to answer the same
question: how can leaders create breakthrough change? That's what
we hope you will get from this book—a new perspective, a new
process, and a new, if not even a bit unusual, set of tools for leading transformation.

Let's begin by diving deeper into how Lowe's achieved the kind
of results described above.

How Did Lowe's Transform?

Although you might be tempted to focus on the technology—the
robots, the exosuits, or a store in space—the transformation at Lowe's
isn't about the technology. Instead, the change occurred through
a human-centered process designed to overcome the key bottlenecks to transformation. What was the process? Forewarning: the
answer may sound a bit outlandish at first. But we are simply applying old tools redesigned in new ways and new tools based on
several decades of behavioral science. We then use these tools to address ancient human challenges, namely, the incrementalism, fear,
and habits that hold organizations back from transformational
change. (For details on these tools, see the sidebar "The Research
Foundations of This Book.")

For example, to develop the tools delivered on AR phones, we
started by assembling Lowe's data about consumer needs and technology trends and then shared this data with a panel of science fiction writers (yes, science fiction, as in *Star Wars*).[8] We then asked
the writers to imagine the near future—five to ten years away—

when Lowe's would solve a critical customer problem using technology. The writers returned with a wild array of stories, complete with dystopian overlords in some cases. But surprisingly, many stories converged around a key theme: using VR and AR to address the challenge of envisioning how to remodel a home and then communicate that vision to others.[9] We then worked, over several rounds of iteration, to develop a strategic narrative about what the future could be. When we say narrative, we mean a real story, one with a dramatic arc, a protagonist (the user), a dilemma (the customer problem), and a resolution. Then we converted the story into a comic book and distributed it to the executives (yes, comic books . . . just imagine handing a comic book to your CEO, who has built a reputation and career as a no-nonsense operator who demands results).

But we didn't stop there. We started building prototypes right away and put high-resolution electroencephalograph (EEG) headsets and eye trackers on customers to understand their reactions to both the stories and the prototypes.[10] Using applied neuroscience, we could see the things users couldn't tell us, for example, how their brains overheated when the users were immersed in VR or how they liked the AR better when the simulation was actually less, rather than more, realistic.[11] Most importantly, we could gather live data on people's reactions and correlate it with a behavioral database to provide data-driven indicators about the best path forward. Along the way, we also intentionally used this information as currency to attract marquee partners such as Google and Microsoft and collaborated with them to provide Lowe's access to their best technology and teams.

Of course, the transformation wasn't devoid of struggle and resistance. Although several visionary senior leaders had championed the change, the organization was just at the beginning of the transformation journey.[12]

For a moment, put yourself back in time to 2012, during the winter of VR, when people remembered VR technology primarily as a failed technology from the 1990s. It was long before people started talking about VR or AR as useful technologies. Kyle had joined Lowe's the year before with a personal goal of trying to test his theories about how to transform the average big company. (Although it's fun to talk about Amazon or Google, it's another matter for a legacy operating company to transform itself.) Thanks to the support of several visionary executives, Kyle had recently gotten his big chance to apply these ideas to transform Lowe's. Using his science fiction approach, he began to prepare to present to the rest of the staff the AR and VR vision he had created.

Kyle had a great deal of trepidation about the upcoming presentation at Lowe's. Experience had taught him about the dangers of presenting an unusual idea that challenges the status quo. Recently, he had presented to a group of executives from across several industries (some details disguised to protect identities) about the possibilities of AR and VR. In the meeting, he had described how AR could change the future of how customers interact with many products and services. As he was standing in front of the group, presenting the possibilities, a senior executive from the construction industry started booing. Loudly.

Surprised, Kyle paused to catch his breath.

Then the executive leaned forward in his chair and in a loud voice said, "No, no, no. Nope." The executive continued: "We studied this exact technology, and it's ten years away from even getting started. This is a dead end."

As people shifted uneasily in their seats, Kyle stood momentarily stunned. The presentation could hardly be going worse, he thought.

Then, recovering, he reached into his backpack and responded, "Well, we've already done it. I have it right here." He pulled out an iPad with an Occipital camera—a new kind of camera that could take the measurements of a space when the instrument was pointed around a room. He demonstrated how he could do just this with the camera and next demonstrated how to view a few preloaded digital objects in the actual room on the iPad. In this way, he showed how a user could envision remodeling a space in real time, instantly visualizing a new couch or refrigerator in their space.[13]

Now the stunned silence seemed to be one of approval. Kyle heard a few *wows*. At the time, few people were talking about AR, and Pokémon Go had not yet been launched. This technology was truly new. The mixed group of executives began to leave their seats to get a closer look. A few tried out the camera, measuring the stage and then placing a digital refrigerator next to the podium to see how it fit in the space. After a few minutes of using the AR device, the attendees retook their seats. Kyle continued presenting, but after the audience had seen how he had turned science fiction into reality, the tone in the room had completely changed.

Fortunately, when Kyle presented the AR and VR project at Lowe's, the presentation went more smoothly, with no one shouting him down. The story gave the leaders a reason to believe in a more attractive possible future, and the comic book helped communicate the big opportunity. The prototyping process, as Kyle described it, would benefit from Lowe's working with *uncommon partners*—organizations that a company might not normally work with, but which could help it move into new areas—and would demonstrate the feasibility of the vision described in the story. The executives wouldn't need to wait for Microsoft or Google to bring the technology to them. Even more audacious: Lowe's could do the work itself!

At the time, Facebook hadn't yet purchased Oculus Rift, and no one was talking about the future of AR or VR. This technology was truly new. The conversation became not about how AR was impossible for a company like Lowe's, but instead about how Lowe's could be the one to lead it. By the end of the process, the Lowe's leadership team was focused on the opportunity: Lowe's could become a different kind of company, one that created the future rather than letting it just happen.

Five years later, mixed-reality devices had become the rage. Oculus Rift had been acquired for $2 billion by Facebook and had since begun selling headsets to consumers. Google Cardboard had made VR accessible to everyone. And Pokémon Go had been downloaded by half a billion people in the first two months of its release and made an average of $2 million a day (and over $1 billion in total) as a free app.[14] In 2017, Michael Porter wrote a *Harvard Business Review* article about how every company needed an AR strategy.[15] But while other companies were scrambling to understand how to use AR or VR in their business, Lowe's was already benefitting from it. The retailer was first in applying AR to the massive home improvement market, partnering with Lenovo and Google to introduce an AR-enabled phone for sale for $500 in stores and online—surprising by any measure—but the "digital power tool" sold out in short order, with little marketing.[16]

Most importantly, as Kyle successfully applied the transformation process repeatedly to more initiatives (specifically, those described at the beginning of this chapter), Lowe's began to transform itself. The ossified operator of the past was quickly becoming an agile competitor that could dream bigger, execute on those dreams, and create its own future. It has since evolved from a home improvement retailer to a purpose-driven, home improvement technology company, officially changing its designation with shareholders and moving into spaces no one would have imagined years ago.

In addition to AR, exosuits, 3-D printing, imaging services, and robots, Lowe's is redefining the idea of stores, home improvement, and home building. For example, could a store be a hybrid between your physical home and a virtual store? Could a store be mobile only? In terms of what home improvement means, could managing apartments be home improvement? Could education be part of home improvement, too? And, for example, could home building products be made directly from recycled materials brought by customers, and could materials be printed onsite instead of shipped from stores?[17] Lowe's teams are energized by their opportunities. In short, Lowe's is undergoing a major transformation to become the kind of company ready for the future. Whether its transformation

The Research Foundations of This Book: A New Behavioral Science of Transformation

This book begins differently than do most books. Although all three authors have PhD training and their recommendations are based on three decades of behavioral research, the book is not an academic's perspective on how to lead change. Instead, the book describes what worked in real organizations to create change and how to repeat it. Thus, our goal is not to create an A-to-Z encyclopedia, a comprehensive handbook of transformation. Nor do we report on the research on transformation. Instead, we hope to give you access to the tools to lead a transformation. We also aim to start a conversation about the new or redesigned tools that are based on behavioral science and that will allow us to finally break through the human barriers to better futures.

To develop the tools we describe here, we drew on the established research, and our own research, across multiple related disciplines. Specifically, we took insights from behavioral economics, psychology, social psychology, applied neuroscience, and innovation.[a] In drawing on these domains, instead of rattling off lists of issues, biases, and limitation (the behavioral sciences alone have identified hundreds of biases and forces affecting our behavior), we focused on the critical behavioral traps we see in the real world—the fear, habits, politics, and incremental thinking that hold organizations back from doing what they say they will do. For example, when we talk about incremental thinking and how to overcome it, we are considering all the literature from psychology (e.g., confirmation bias, relatedness bias, and anchoring), neuroscience (e.g., neural responses to risk and uncertainty and neural mechanisms of creativity), and innovation (e.g., incremental innovation and ideation).

In light of this research (including our own contributions to these fields), we conducted additional research directly related to the ideas in the book. For example, we examined the Global 500 companies and their stated missions to understand if and how they use any form of narrative, as described in the book. We also conducted studies on other topics in this book, such as how to generate a greater number of novel ideas, how stories influence persuasion, and which media are the most persuasive. Finally, we designed and tested the tools in the book. For example, Thomas is perhaps the world's foremost expert on neuroprototyping (i.e., the use of applied neuroscience tools to understand how people respond at a neural level to new products), having developed some of the most relevant applications of neuroscience to innovation and transformation problems.

But instead of reporting these studies as a listicle of findings, we acknowledge this research and then focus on how to use the tools developed to lead transformation. Although some of the names and situations are disguised to protect identities, we describe tools that we have tested and used in real organizations to overcome the common barriers to transformation. We openly acknowledge that these tools are not fail-proof, comprehensive, or relevant to every situation. No tools are. Instead, they simply address the behavioral traps we have identified as the most challenging, and they have worked for us.

Throughout the book, various endnotes cite the research underlying these tools, and sidebars dig deeper into the relevant research and mechanisms. A list of foundational readings is also included at the end of the book. The "Digital Toolbox" sections in each chapter present an online repository of tools, templates, and training that you can use or develop to fit your situation as you apply these ideas in your own organization.

Finally, the opportunities to further develop the science of transformation are also the reason we are creating the Transformation Lab, an interdisciplinary center to explore and design the tools we need to navigate the future. Because of the exponential growth in computing power, we are entering an era of unprecedented change and uncertainty. Many of the tools designed for a previous era of relative organizational and economic stability, an era of coordination and control, will fail in the era of uncertainty, which requires adaptation and change. The Transformation Lab is dedicated to discovering, encouraging, redesigning, and sharing the theories, frameworks, processes, and tools for a world of uncertainty.

This book is the first step in the effort to shape this new body of work.

a. For behavioral economics, psychology, and social psychology, see Dan Ariely, *Predictably Irrational: The Hidden Forces That Shape Our Decisions* (New York: Harper-Collins, 2009); Daniel Kahneman, *Thinking, Fast and Slow* (New York: Macmillan, 2011); Richard H. Thaler, *Misbehaving: The Making of Behavioral Economics* (New York: W.W. Norton & Company, 2016); and Lee Ross and Richard Nisbett, *The Person and the Situation: Perspectives of Social Psychology* (London: Pinter and Martin, 2011). For applied neuroscience, see Joseph LeDoux, *The Emotional Brain: The Mysterious Underpinnings of Emotional Life* (New York: Simon & Schuster, 1998); Antonio Damasio, *Descartes' Error: Emotion, Reason, and the Human Brain* (New York: Penguin, 2005), for summaries; and Eric R. Kandel, ed., *Principles of Neuroscience*, 5th ed. (New York: McGraw-Hill Education/Medical, 2012). For innovation, see Nathan Furr and Jeffrey H. Dyer, *The Innovator's Method: Bringing the Lean Startup into Your Organization* (Boston: Harvard Business Review Press, 2014); Jeffrey H. Dyer, Hal Gregersen, and Clayton M. Christensen, *The Innovator's DNA: Mastering the Five Skills of Disruptive Innovators* (Boston: Harvard Business Review Press, 2011); and Clayton M. Christensen, *The Innovator's Dilemma: When New Technologies Cause Great Firms to Fail* (Boston: Harvard Business Review Press, 2016).

continues will depend, in part, on applying the ideas described in this book.

Each technological and behavioral change was the outcome of a process that Kyle applied over and over to effect a true transformation at Lowe's. In that fateful meeting with Lowe's executives, when Kyle showed them the comic book, the executives (and Lowe's) were transformed. Kyle had applied the transformation process to create a bigger vision for the future and then to build that future. This transformation process invited resisters to jump on board and allowed the organization to suspend disbelief long enough to make a change.

The transformation did not result from an overarching mandate to change, followed by a roster of initiatives executed with militaristic force. Instead, the transformation occurred through the repetition of the process described in this book, building up the organization's confidence and capabilities until, through many small-*t* transformations, Lowe's made a big-*T* transformation. The core of the business continues to grow, and Lowe's is ready for the future. Although technology played a role in Lowe's transformation, it does not play a role in every transformation, and it is not the main character of the story. Instead, the real crux of the transformation depended on something much more common and fundamental: a set of tools to overcome the common behavioral barriers to transformation.

The Transformation Process: Three Steps to Take Charge of Your Company's Future

The process we describe for tackling some of the most difficult human limitations to transformation has three steps, all of which are based on behavioral science (e.g., psychology and neuroscience) (figure 1-1). Great transformers from the past—people who understood intuitively how to apply these ideas—often used these tools or elements of them. We simply describe the tools more concretely and how to use them.

Envisioning the Future: Using Science Fiction and Strategic Narrative

One of the biggest limitations to creating the future is the human tendency toward narrow thinking, or seeing only incremental improvements to the status quo. In contrast, we admire innovators like Elon Musk or Jeff Bezos precisely because they dream bigger, dare bigger, and then inspire those around them to change the world. When we interviewed Musk and his team at Tesla, what surprised

FIGURE 1-1

Leading transformation: three interrelated and iterative steps

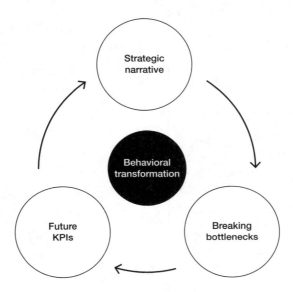

Note: KPIs, key performance indicators

us most was how Musk's vision to change the world to a renewable, electric vehicle future had infected everyone at the company. Common engineers, assembly-line workers, and even custodians truly believe they are changing the world, not just making cars. One leader told us confidentially, "We don't have the best engineers in the world, but they believe in what we are doing so much, we can do amazing things with them." How can we do the same thing in the organizations we lead? How can we break free of incrementalism, dream bigger, and inspire people to follow us?

Our framework begins with a *strategic narrative* about a possible future. The narrative's content and structure inspires people, dispels disbelief, and compels transformation. Before you dismiss this step as old news, consider that although business leaders talk about stories in big organizations, most leaders really have no clue about how to use them properly. In our analysis of Global 500 companies, less than 10 percent of companies appeared to have any meaningful story, and fewer used it well. But stories are one of humankind's oldest and most powerful tools. Since the time when we humans gathered around the fire (and still do), stories have opened our eyes to what is possible, suspended our disbelief, and stirred our hearts into action. The power of story has its roots in evolutionary psychology: recent neuroscience research reveals that stories release a rush of neurochemicals that can literally sync people's brains with one another and motivate action.[18] When used properly, a story can help people see the future and can transform them from adversaries into advocates working hard to create that future.

In our transformation process, we focus on constructing strategic narratives based on a radical reenvisioning of what is possible. We use tools like *speculative fiction* to help us break the bonds of incrementalism and then to create a narrative that truly motivates and inspires those around us. The resulting story involves a protagonist, a dilemma, and a resolution, all built into a narrative arc that gives us reason to believe. We then find a compelling way of telling the story—a *dramatic medium* such as comics, videos, or even hip-hop (figure 1-2). Ultimately, what matters is finding a way of storytelling that overcomes your audience's natural resistance. Our research reveals that the visual format often helps people suspend their critical mind and engage with the emotion of the story. In chapter 2, we will show you how to create a story that can inspire commitment and change necessary to take charge of your future.

Breaking Bottlenecks: Using Decision Maps and Archetypes

We aren't the first people to talk about telling a powerful story (although we may be the first to use science fiction writers and comic books in the C-suite), but many people who have created stories have still wrecked on the rocks of routine. Developing the story may be the easier part. Navigating the rat's nest of motivations, politics, and routines in any big company may be the hardest part. Few sta-

FIGURE 1-2

Sample narrative comic

Source: Courtesy Uncommon Partners.

tistics exist to reveal how many initiatives are derailed by the decision bottlenecks in an organization, but in a recent survey, 72 percent of senior executives believed that bad strategic decisions were as frequent as, or more frequent than, good decisions in their organizations.[19]

There is no simple formula to overcome these challenges, but by applying tools rooted in behavioral science, you can find better ways to identify and break the bottlenecks. These tools are the focus of chapter 3. To start breaking these bottlenecks, we begin by asking a simple question: what kind of organization do you work in? This often-unasked question reveals deep insights about what the organization values and the organization's dominant *nomenclature*, or *language*, required to communicate and get things done. Then we map out the informal and formal decision process by creating a *decision bottleneck map*. Next we identify the individual *archetypes*—the primary roles that decision makers play—and where they sit in the key decision holdups. Using this critical information, we can look at the organization's habits and use them as *bottleneck breakers* to facilitate a transformation.

We'll describe several common habits of organizations, but one of the most underappreciated involves a company's tendency to overlook abundance. For example, Lowe's initially overlooked the value of the millions of customers walking into its stores wanting to learn—the ideal environment for experimenting with new technologies. But through our guidance, Lowe's learned to recognize the value of this abundance and turn it into a currency to attract some of the world's leading partners, such as Microsoft and Google.

Navigating the Unknown: Using Applied Neuroscience and Future Key Performance Indicators (fKPIs)

Doing something new, whether it be transformation or innovation, almost always creates fear and resistance. Voltaire, the French philosopher, once wrote, "Our wretched species is so made that those who walk on the well-trodden path always throw stones at those who are showing a new road."[20] In addition to encountering resistance from others, when you pioneer into new territory, you rarely see many signposts that you are heading in the right direction. You are the one blazing the trail. Thus, you have few data points to reinforce your own confidence that you are on the right track.

To overcome the fear that accompanies doing something new, you need data-driven indicators that you are on course, both to guide your choices and to create confidence among those you lead. Unfortunately, most of the measurement tools available are built to assess past performance and so are unreliable indicators of an uncertain future. For example, tools like focus groups or customer feedback can be notoriously dangerous when you are designing new-to-the-world products. Gianfranco Zaccai, who developed the Aeron chair, the Reebok Pump, and the Swiffer, used to say, "I've never seen innovation come out of a focus group."[21]

To move into the future, we need new tools and measures to accurately understand what direction to go. Chapter 4 shows how to use artifact trails, experimental design, and data-driven indicators to obtain signposts as you break new territory. You also learn how to create confidence in those around you so that they are inspired to join you. Specifically, we start by identifying the end goal, then work backward to define an *artifact trail*—the series of small, observable activities and prototypes that can act as small wins to keep enthusiasm high. We then define the *future key performance indicators* (fKPIs, where the lowercase *f* represents the function of how you create the future) and the experimental design needed to reliably generate defensible measures of the direction you are going. Typically, we use a tool like the *experimental design canvas*, described in the book, to choose the fKPIs needed to navigate the future. Then we apply the best tools we can find to generate these fKPIs.

Our favorite tool, and perhaps the most valuable one, to navigate the unknown is *applied neuroscience*. This tool generates data that can reveal what people don't even know about themselves. To use applied neuroscience for transformation, we used four research-based measures—engagement, emotion, overload, and attention—which we correlate to actual behaviors to predict the best path forward.[22] We compiled this data to help Lowe's choose between mixed reality, VR, and AR—and the decision helped the company collaborate in the launch of one of the first commercially available AR phones, which we described earlier. Although neuroscience may be the Ferrari of experimental design tools and remarkably inexpensive when sourced from a reliable vendor, the key is not the neuroscience. Instead, the focus is on designing new fKPIs to overcome fear and give you the confidence to move into the future.

Taking Charge of Your Future

In this book, we describe some of the many possible tools for leading transformation by addressing the ultimate bottleneck, the human element of transformation. Don't be confused by the technologies, the science fiction, or the comics. What we care about is behavior change. We have applied these same ideas at companies like Pepsi, where there was little technology involved—just transformation. Similarly, we applied the tools at Svensk Film, to help it explore how to transform itself from a film company that owns cinemas and produces movies to a company that creates experiences and inspires passion, an emotion the company can now objectively measure using applied neuroscience and use as a guide on its journey. Ultimately, the transformation process is designed to help people overcome the incrementalism, routine, and fear that holds back transformation. To help you apply the transformation process, we will describe how to create strategic narratives, break bottlenecks, and create fKPIs that allow you to chart a real path to an exciting future. We will also emphasize the Trojan horse approach to transformation: rather than attacking transformation head-on, we propose that you create many small, realizable transformations that will add up to a major transformation—the same way that Lowe's built up many small-t changes that ultimately added up to a big-T transformation.

We recognize that the approach in this book isn't the only road to transformation and that we don't describe all the available tools. We welcome the addition of new tools, of which there will be many more. All of us are at the beginning of a conversation, not at the end of it. Many of you will no doubt develop even better tools to address the behavioral limitations described here or new tools to address the barriers we have not addressed.

In closing, we are certain of one thing: the future, as a fixed destination to be reached at some impending date, does not actually exist. Although you may pay smart consultants to help you understand that future, they can't tell you what it will be either, because no one knows the future. They can't know the future, because there is no predetermined future out there other than the one you create!

Ultimately, this book is about recognizing this simple idea: that you can envision the future you want to create, and then by working with these tools, in collaboration with uncommon partners, you can take charge of the future for your organization. Of course, there are constraints. You cannot wave a magic wand. But the future only happens when someone takes action and creates it. If we learn one thing from innovators like Musk, Bezos, or Jobs, it's that they had the gumption to create the future they imagined. So if someone is going to create the future, why not you? You can take charge of your future and shape it in the direction you hope it will go.

As more of us realize this point, the future will become ever more dynamic. For those who are trying to hide in the old, walled gardens of supposed competitive advantage, this new approach will feel like a threat and will create unbearable uncertainty. But uncertainty is only one side of the coin—the side we see when others seem to be changing the world in which we live. The other side of the coin is possibility—the possibility that as the barriers to participate, create, and interact come down, the possible new futures we can create together will only increase. This book is about taking charge of your future.

TWO

Envisioning the Future

Using Science Fiction and Strategic Narratives to Create a Compelling Story

In 1981, Harvard psychologist Ellen Langer literally turned back time using a story. One autumn day, she welcomed eight men in their seventies to a retreat center in New Hampshire. Several of the men struggled getting off the bus with their suitcases and canes, and some men were stooped with arthritis. As the first man stepped inside, something strange happened. He paused, shocked and puzzled. Inside, the black-and-white television blared out news about Wilt Chamberlain's recent 1959 visit to Moscow with the Harlem Globetrotters. The bulletin board at the retreat center displayed the retreat participant's picture from twenty-two years earlier. Next to it was pinned an announcement: the center would be showing Jimmy Stewart's new release, *Anatomy of a Murder*. But the movie had been produced in 1959, not the present year of 1981. After a moment, he stepped all the way through the door and was greeted by a friendly staff member wearing a distinctly 1950s skirt. As the other men gathered around him, the retreat director reminded the men that they should only talk about their lives and careers in 1959, using the present tense. Then, ignoring the obvious canes and stooped backs, she instructed the men that they should carry their own bags upstairs and that, afterward, they could join the group for drinks and a predinner discussion about the recent US satellite launch, the Explorer 1, which had just reached space the year before . . . in 1958.

As the men set aside their canes and carried their own bags upstairs, something imperceptible began to change. For five more days, the men lived in the time machine, talking and living as if it were twenty-two years earlier. At the end of the retreat, not only did they report feeling younger, but they also acted younger: when measured, they were more flexible, had greater dexterity in their hands, sat taller, and had better eyesight. As they waited for the bus to take them back home, these same older men who had walked into the center tentatively and slowly with their canes now walked out without canes. They even started an impromptu touch-football game in the parking lot while they waited. Overall, the results were so profound, and the sample so small, that Langer never published the study in an academic journal, fearing that it would be rejected as outright unbelievable.[1]

Instead of publishing the experiment, she conducted a battery of more-conservative studies that demonstrate something we know intuitively to be true—the power of stories to change how we see the world or ourselves. For example, in one study, a hotel's housekeeping staff members who initially complained that they had no time for exercise were told that the surgeon general had recently designated their work as strenuous exercise. Almost immediately, these workers started to lose weight and experienced lower blood pressure, whereas the control group that was told nothing experienced no changes.[2]

In another study, while people slept, their clocks were manipulated to run two hours slower or faster than the time displayed. But when these participants were given tasks to test their ability, they performed according to how much sleep they thought they received, not how much they actually slept.[3] In another study, also manipulating the clocks, people with type 2 diabetes experienced glucose highs and lows that corresponded with the time they thought it was, not with the actual time.[4]

Although Langer's research has drawn both praise and criticism, it reveals the power of the stories we tell to literally change how we see the world and what we can do. Indeed, a story that Einstein told himself—about what it would be like to ride a beam of light versus watch the beam of light on earth—is what led him to the theory of general relativity, which reset the course of physics.

The Core Dilemma: Incremental Thinking

Although it is easy to be inspired by the power of a story to turn back time or make scientific breakthroughs, the other side of the coin revealed by Langer's research is the power of the biases that hold us back. Without our ever realizing it, these stories and patterns limit our thinking and actions. In particular, the tendency toward incremental thinking—to see and act on what is nearby, easy to access, and familiar rather than what is possible—may be the first obstacle to overcome when we try to change.

Thomas learned about the problems of incremental thinking first-hand in the neurological wards at Copenhagen University Hospital. He was treating patients who had had strokes to their right parietal cortex, the area of the brain slightly above the ear. Such strokes often lead to paralysis in the left side of the body and face (in the brain, things cross over so that the left side of the body is controlled by the right side of the brain, and vice versa). Interestingly, other strange things often happen in these cases. In the ward, these patients run into things with their left hands, left legs, and left sides of their wheelchairs, as if they were blind. The male patients do not shave on the left sides of their faces. Patients rarely put on the left sides of their clothes. They complain about getting less food than all the other patients do—they only see one side of their plates. But they are not blind. They can physically see what's on the left-hand side of their bodies. Rather, they simply neglect this side. They have lost the ability to pay attention to whatever exists to their left side, both their external surroundings and themselves. In medical terms, it's called *unilateral neglect*—these patients literally neglect one side of their entire life.

Although such behavior may seem extreme, healthy individuals—you and the rest of us—aren't so different. Indeed, we all suffer from some kind of unilateral neglect because we are unaware of our own limitations, the most critical limit being our tendency to see only what is close at hand instead of what is possible. Said differently, we neglect the more distant possibilities, even though these may be the most interesting and valuable opportunities available to us. There are many reasons for this limitation, not just brain damage in the form of unilateral neglect. Indeed, prior research has revealed an entire class of biases related to our tendency to see what is easy to see; these biases go by names such as functional fixedness, confirmation bias, recency bias, and intertemporal choice bias.[5]

To understand the pernicious pervasiveness of these biases, consider the implications of one study about functional fixedness—the tendency to see things as they currently are. Participants were given a problem whose solution required a wire (imagine using a wire to reset an electrical device). When given a stack of paper and a paperclip, most participants can solve the problem. But when given a stack of paper held together by a paper clip, most people failed to figure out that they could have used the paper clip as a wire.[6] Similarly, in a different study about confirmation bias—the tendency to listen only to evidence that supports our current views—72 percent of participants in a mock trial voted for a guilty verdict because of an eyewitness account. But when those same participants were told, after delivering their verdict, that the eyewitness was blind and so couldn't have seen the crime, only 4 percent of the jurors changed their vote.[7] Similarly, we tend to pay attend to recent data more than distant data (recency bias). And we have a hard time making good decisions that have an impact in the future; instead, we are biased to the here and now (intertemporal choice bias). In sum, there are many reasons why we focus on what is near at hand, rather than on more distant, potentially more valuable possibilities.

The Need: New Tools to Create Grand Visions

Rather than endlessly catalog the biases that limit people's ability to see outside the small box of the everyday, we'll simply say that people need new tools to break free of incrementalism and to envision what's possible. In recent years, several new tools have appeared, particularly in the innovation realm. Frameworks like design thinking help innovators develop customer empathy, and lean startup helps innovators run rapid, rigorous experiments to test critical hypotheses. But these valuable tools aren't designed to overcome the core psychological biases that hold us back. Consequently, they won't necessarily help us break free of incrementalism. Ask yourself, will observing customers use phones, or A/B testing a web page, lead to SpaceX or the next transistor? Most likely not. These new frameworks, although very helpful for more-incremental innovation activities, are not built to see the distances needed for a grand vision—one that can change your organization or the world (figure 2-1). To see further, to make big leaps, we need a new approach. Ironically, we found a way to use old tools in new ways as well as new tools that are specifically targeted to overcome the hidden biases and help us break free to create inspiring new futures.

The Process: How to Create the Future Using Science Fiction and Narrative

Anyone who has tried to lead change in a big company knows how hard it is to move from meetings to action. Although everyone may

FIGURE 2-1

Enhancing adaptability

Exponential thinking and adaptability: mindset, tools, and network

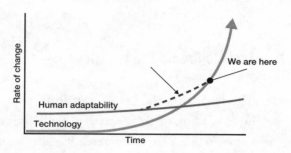

Source: Courtesy Robert Nail, Singularity University.

nod their heads in the meeting, creating real behavior change is an entirely different matter. There are several prescribed remedies, and we have tried them all, including preselling the results, giving leaders information about our personal experience with the problem, and using data. But these tactics rarely produced behavior change. One particular meeting stands out: In desperation to communicate his message, Kyle read and applied the advice of a former P&G executive who suggested that the presenter read the headlines of each slide and ensure that they tell a story. Kyle diligently applied the advice and tried to convince the audience, but by the end of the presentation and an afternoon of debate, there was no more behavior change than when he started. The research, preselling, personal experience, and even the story hadn't worked. Or, more accurately, what we call a story in the business world—often just a chronological series of events—hadn't worked. In such a "story" there are no characters, no plot, no conflict, no resolution. Nothing to make you believe. Nothing to inspire change. Truthfully, typical business tales are not real stories.

Real stories are something different. They have characters, conflict, plot, and resolution; they start movements and wars. Real stories are our oldest and most powerful tool. But storytelling wasn't working in big companies. Storytelling is more than a chronological list of events. It should change how you view the world and even help you imagine future worlds.

After years of failed presentations across multiple organizations, Kyle read a book that inspired him. The book described how Michael Crichton had written the science fiction novel *Jurassic Park*, which became an international bestseller and spawned films that have been enjoyed by successive generations of children. The book describes how Crichton developed *Jurassic Park* by visiting the local library and submersing himself in the latest writing on bioengineering, paleontology, archeology, radiocarbon dating, and related technologies and then writing a story about a possible future and its implications. In effect, Crichton had synthesized contemporary data and predicted a plausible future and, in some ways, a not-too-distant future. (In fact, a team at Harvard recently started trying to bring back wooly mammoths through the CRISPR gene-editing technique.)[8]

As Kyle surveyed the incremental innovation efforts at every big company around him, he asked himself, Could we use science fiction to envision a more radical future? Moreover, could we use real stories to motivate the executives to take committed action? Kyle shared his frustrations with his leader at Lowe's, who, believing they should try something different if they wanted to create the future, gave Kyle permission to try it. However, frankly, he probably had no idea how wild Kyle's idea would be![9] He started by assembling Lowe's data about customer experiences and external reports about technology trends from companies like Gartner and Forrester and then gave this data to a panel of five science fiction writers.[10] He asked them to write a story about what the future could be like in five to ten years, with real customers at the center of the story. Surprisingly, three of the five stories came back with narratives about using immersive reality (e.g., AR and VR) to envision how to improve their homes. (The fourth story was mainly about a dystopian overlord, and the fifth future was no different from today.)

Using these stories, Kyle worked with the best storyteller of the group and, over multiple iterations, developed a single story of how immersive reality might help customers envision how to remodel their homes. He then captured this story in a few pages—the first draft was only about ten pages long. But the story had emotional power because it described real people trying to solve a meaningful dilemma. The early story even had a few watercolor illustrations (see figure 2-2 for an example).

Finally, the time came to share the story with the executives in Kyle's business unit. The night beforehand, as Kyle and his boss were traveling to meet with the rest of the division, the boss suggested they pick out a movie to watch together. "What about *Iron Man*?" Kyle suggested. Without hesitating, his boss responded flatly, "I hate science fiction. Let's watch something else." In an instant, Kyle felt like an idiot. The next morning, he was going to present science

FIGURE 2-2

First watercolor of a mixed-reality story

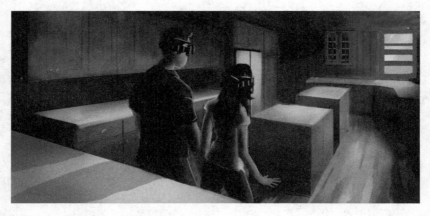

Source: www.lowesinnovationlabs.com/narrative.

fiction not only to his boss but also his entire business unit. Suddenly, he began to dread his bold experiment.

But the next morning, Kyle stood up anyway in front of the very same boss and other executives and described the process—curated data, science fiction, strategic narratives, and (the most unbelievable of all) comic books to tell the story. There were a few laughs around the room and many amused smiles. But then Kyle passed out the story, a Word document with a few images inserted (figure 2-2 shows one of the first watercolors). The story itself describes a young couple struggling to maintain an aging home. They love the house, which they purchased out of their savings, and its history (it was originally built by a war veteran). But as they try to stay on top of the repairs, they know they need to update the house. But how? They each have a different vision, they are scared to make the wrong choice and waste their savings, and they struggle to communicate their vision to a contractor. But when they come to Lowe's, they use immersive technology to envision what their home could be, to make decisions together, and to guide the contractor in the right direction.

At the time, AR and VR weren't as popular as they are today. Oculus Rift wouldn't even be founded until a few months later, and no one was talking about the technology. But when the executives in the room read the story about how a couple could use these futuristic technologies to create a place they love, the entire tenor of the room changed. The skepticism disappeared. The risk aversion evaporated. The hedging and the doubt and the "we can't do this, because we aren't a tech company" and all the related excuses disappeared. In its place was enthusiasm and urgency. The conversation went from "we can't do this" to "we have to do this."

When the meeting ended, the head of international insisted that this idea needed to be accelerated to a group of forty-five top executives leading the entire company. In the intervening six weeks, Kyle worked furiously to create a comic book that told the story. He also laid out the artifact trail to get there and started developing prototypes (see chapters 3 and 4). The first mixed-reality prototypes were crude by today's standards. For example, one version consisted of an iPad that you could point at a QR code placed in a physical room and then view a dozen or so digital objects superimposed onto the photo view of the room, in the spot where you had placed the QR code marker.[11]

The team learned an incredible amount from the six weeks of prototyping. First, the prototype absolutely captured the imagination of customers. A customer would visit the store in the morning and, by midday, would return with a gaggle of friends and family. Although the prototype was up for just five days, the word-of-mouth reaction had led to incredible in-store traffic. Second, even though the team was using generic digital objects (e.g., a generic bathtub or light) in the mixed-reality experiments, customers were asking to buy the objects. Finally, the iPad version that allowed you to interact with the room you were facing proved much more interesting to people. The success of the iPad version led Kyle to track down a startup called Occipital—a Kickstarter success that had made a splash with a 3-D depth-sensing camera. (At the time, Occipital's prototype wasn't much more than a Microsoft Kinect camera paired with software that allowed you to measure a room.) Despite the attention being showered on Occipital, Kyle successfully tracked the company down at CES's technology show and, over nine hours, persuaded the startup to give him one of three demo devices in existence. The persistence paid off. Both the strategic narrative and making it real helped convince skeptics that they could do it. (The importance of making the future real and tangible is discussed later in the book.)

Most importantly, the strategic narrative helped the company move from seeing mostly incremental opportunities to envisioning a whole new set of possibilities and then sustaining a commitment to create those possibilities. This commitment allowed Lowe's to persist through the trough of disillusionment that accompanies most radical changes (figure 2-3). In this trough, most organizations retreat to whatever is at hand and familiar. As a result, they never make it to the other side. But those that persist in the right way (using low-cost experimentation, not bet-the-farm gambles) are those that are ready when disruptions hit. But it takes both vision and commitment to get through disillusionment. Because Lowe's used strategic narrative to persist through discouraging times, the company was ready when, five years later, mixed reality became a huge market.

Kyle's experience at Lowe's illustrates the first step in the process— breaking free of incrementalism to create the vision and belief in the possible future. In this first step, you use science fiction, strategic narrative, and graphic novels (or another vivid storytelling medium) to break free of incrementalism, see valuable new possibilities, and inspire others to join. Below, we describe these three tools, why they work, and how to use them. Although we focus on Lowe's for the sake of a unifying example, we have also applied these tools to

FIGURE 2-3

Sample comic panel

Source: Courtesy Uncommon Partners.

nontechnology transformations at companies such as Pepsi. For example, as Pepsi moves to become a nutrition-focused organization, they need new ways to build empathy with their changing consumer audience. We have used the strategic narrative process not to imagine a future with VR or robots, but instead how it can help individual customers make the meaningful, healthy changes they want. The new strategic narratives have real impact, helping leaders at Pepsi see where to go and have the motivation to make meaningful changes. Similarly, we have applied this tool at other organizations, some of whom we can describe and others which we cannot. But we will describe the tools you can use to replicate the process yourself.

Tool: Science Fiction

Many people mistakenly see science fiction as the realm of nerds. Few people realize how important science fiction is to the world in which we now live and the language we use every day. For example, without thinking much about it, we use terms like *reality distortion field*, *warp speed*, *the matrix*, and *mother ship*, all drawn from science fiction. Similarly, many of our most notable technologies have been inspired first by science fiction. For example, early sci-fi authors inspired technologies such as the submarine (Jules Verne), the cell phone (Gene Roddenberry and other writers of *Star Trek*), robots (Karel Capek), Taser (Tom Swift adventure series), self-driving cars (Isaac Asimov), earbuds (Ray Bradbury), and atomic power (H. G. Wells).[12] Indeed, many argue that science fiction underpins the entire culture of Silicon Valley and the technology revolution created there. For example, many in Silicon Valley credit the novel *Snow Crash* with inspiring the modern applications of the internet and *Star Trek* for Amazon's Alexa, and Elon Musk says that Isaac Asimov's Foundation series motivated him to develop commercial space travel.[13]

Phil Libin, cofounder of Evernote and All Turtles, is a startup investor and an adjunct instructor at Stanford. Teaching a course on science fiction and Silicon Valley, Libin argues that science fiction played a fundamental role in his life and the broader Silicon Valley. About he and his colleagues in Silicon Valley, he says, "we don't see science fiction as a prediction. Science fiction authors wrote about it, but we built it. It's less prophecy and more our belief that we have to build the world we want."[14] For example, Evernote— the massively popular note-taking software valued at more than $1 billion at its height—was inspired by the augmentation of human intelligence with technology portrayed in the novel *Dune*. Inspired by the novel, he and his cofounders similarly asked, "How could we use technology to augment our intelligence today?" Their answer was a hyper-facile note-taking software that would allow you to augment your memory. "We proactively chose to build that technology based on the novel *Dune*," he said.

Although science fiction has sometimes been relegated to the realm of geeks, movies, or Silicon Valley, it shouldn't be. This genre has special power to help us pull off our blinders and envision other potential futures.[15] Ursula Le Guin, one of the most influential science fiction authors of our time, wrote that "To me the important thing is not to offer any specific hope of betterment but, by offering an imagined but persuasive alternative reality, to dislodge my mind, and so the reader's mind, from the lazy, timorous habit of thinking that the way we live now is the only way people can live."[16] In summary, science fiction can be a tool to break the bonds of incrementalism and to imagine other possibilities. The creative genre can help us dream bigger.

Science fiction inspires us for several reasons. First, it encourages us to imagine—even demands that we imagine—a different but possible future. Second, good science fiction takes into account the human elements of technology and change and wrestles with its implications. Thus, the good stories are less about the technology and more about the human problems that technology reveals or solves. Together these elements—the abilities both to see further and to ask what problems could be solved—can help us break free of the biases that trap us in incremental thinking and can let us envision believable, valuable new futures. As Libin argues, "science fiction can provide a kind of rigorous optimism" needed to see and create the future. "Ultimately, some people think the world can be improved and it is your job to improve it. But you have to do it in a pragmatic way. There's no magic. Science fiction just provides the inspiration, and then you make a rigorous plan and go for it."[17]

How to Use Science Fiction

Science fiction, or what we often call *speculative organizational fiction*, is a tool to break free of the way you see your organization and to dream bigger. Using your existing data as a foundation, writers can help you see what else might be possible. In this section, we will try to systematically describe what we do, so that you can replicate it. But we do so with a bit of hesitancy—using science fiction is always a highly rigorous melding of art and science. Therefore, we suggest you try the following steps.

1. *Curate the data.* Assemble a curated set of customer and technology data to use as the raw materials that inspire your writers.[18]

   - Do use real data from previous projects, qualitative and quantitative studies, and third-party studies on technology trends. For example, when asked to write the Lowe's story, writers were given internal Lowe's data about customer satisfaction, including customer interviews about issues such as what they liked and disliked about retail interactions. Writers were also given files on some internal innovation projects that had failed. Finally, they were

given data on technology trends from third-party researchers like Forrester or Gartner.

- Conduct in-depth interviews with experts, executives,
and thought leaders in the company, both to understand
the needs of leaders and the inspiration of thought leaders. Provide these insights to the writers as well, and
use them as a compass in the development of your
project.

- Put together a nondisclosure agreement (NDA) if some of
the data is sensitive, but keep the document simple.

2. *Assemble a panel of writers.* Find five good storytellers, and
set them to work independently on a short story (around ten
pages) about what the future could look like in the next five
to ten years, in light of the data (see the sidebar "How to
Find and Contract with Science Fiction Writers").

- Select writers who are good storytellers. You can assess
this ability by looking at some of their prior work. For example, does the plot catch you? Can they create characters
you care about?

- Frame the purpose of the project. We tell writers that they
aren't writing a corporate shill piece. Nor are they writing
classical science fiction (if you tell them to write science
fiction, you might receive dark stories filled with robot
overlords). Instead, we tell them we are creating speculative organizational fiction, like the movies *Back to the
Future* or *Minority Report*, but for organizations. They almost always quickly understand.

- Don't assume you know whether writers want credit for
their work. Some do, some don't want credit. Be prepared
to discuss your expectations.

- Don't try to force the hands of the writers. Let them pull the insights from the data. Their stories might surprise you. In fact, you could almost say the goal is to be surprised. For example, although mixed-reality technologies were discussed in only about 0.1 percent of the curated data we gave to the writers, three of the five writers discussed the use of mixed reality. We find that often three of the five writers come up with similar themes.

- Remind them to tell a story with the customer at the center. As we will discuss, true narratives have a narrative arc with characters, conflict, and resolution.

- Give them a deadline, about six to eight weeks, at which point you want to check in on a draft of the project to make sure they are going down the right path.

- Tell the writers that you are working with other writers and that in later rounds you will work with one of them to synthesize the stories into a single narrative.

- Use their language (use terms like *projects, drafts*, and *revisions*), not your own peculiar corporate or startup language.

3. *Synthesize the stories.* When you get the stories back, expect to find a lot of variety (this is good), but look for common themes as you iterate to a single story.

   - Be methodical in looking at the themes that arise in the first round. We often code the key themes using numbers, tally the themes, and then rank them according to the number of times they appear and their importance to the organization.

   - Don't work with the author of the story with the most technical insight. Rather, work with the best storyteller (i.e., the person best at creating a narrative arc). Discuss

How to Find and Contract with Science Fiction Writers

Most of us aren't regularly hanging out with many science fiction writers, so where do you find them? First, we acknowledge that it can take some effort to get started. Start with writers' associations. For example, the Science Fiction and Fantasy Writers of America (SFWA) can be a great resource because it is an industry association of published authors, rather than people who say they want to write science fiction but who have no experience. On the SFWA website, you can find authors and read their work.

When we started, we read stories posted online, looking for authors whose work felt authentic and who could create a strong plot or characters we cared about. We also wanted writers who were not too bombastic (for whom everything is exploding and falling apart). We then emailed or phoned these authors. When we found someone who would talk to us, but who didn't want to do the work, we asked for recommendations of three people who were good. The SFWA is a network, and the best way to navigate it is with the help of insiders.

Whenever we engage a writer, we contract with the person on terms that may vary, depending on the project scope. For example, we may need a first draft plus three revisions, with options to flex the work up or down as needed. We also have writers sign documents, primarily an NDA and a creative license that allows us to use what they write however we want. Part of the agreement entails specifying how the work may be shared externally. Typically, we identify one or two frames or scenes that could be used to explain concepts to media, or to allow the artist to build a portfolio. We usually do not publish the entire narrative, since that would mean sharing our strategy! Finally, we understand that many authors may or may not want their name attached to the work, so we check their preferences in advance.

Help Finding Writers

Finding good writers who understand the process and thus are easy to work with can save you an incredible amount of time and lead to much better results. If you want a shortcut to finding writers who understand the process already, on our website, leadingtransformationbook .com, we provide some connections to certified writers whom we have worked with or taught.

the key themes from the stories, and work with the writer to synthesize a new story.

- Expect to iterate. We went through ten rounds on this first story.

- Don't be afraid to press the restart button. If no themes or too many conflicting themes emerge, or the majority of the stories just seem off, restart the process from the beginning with a new set of writers.

Caveats and Alternatives: Working without Science Fiction

Perhaps you can't find a science fiction writer, or perhaps you really do hate science fiction. You can use alternatives—other writers, thought partners, analogies, and so forth. But the underlying principle is find a tool that helps you break free of the incrementalism that traps us all. To move away from incrementalism, it helps to get outside the walls of your own organization and, probably, outside the walls of your industry. In applying alternatives, you are looking for people and organizations that are very different from you. You then seek inspiration by considering how they might do what you do differently.

As one alternative to science fiction, you can use analogs and ant-onym analogies (explained below), to think differently about your possibilities. As an example of how to use analogies, start by iden-tifying several admirable organizations that are different from your organization and ask two questions: How would they do an activ-ity that you're considering? How would they *not* do it? So, for ex-ample, how would Amazon do your same activity? What would it not do? What about Apple, Google, 3M, Tesla, the Bill & Melinda Gates Foundation, or any other number of organizations that are different from you?

Once you get a list of ideas from your analogs (approaches you would be likely to try), you can try the antonym analogies (ap-proaches you should avoid). For example, how would Amazon *never* do it? You may also challenge yourself with another question: How would a startup do it? Or, if we were to rebuild our business from the ground up today, how would we do it? Once you've gener-ated some ideas with analogs and antonym analogies, you can start to synthesize the opportunities you've identified into a story.

Tool: Strategic Narrative

In 2017, we created a very unusual event, bringing together rappers like MC Lyte, Doug E. Fresh, and Stretch Armstrong, with some uncommon partners, including the US Department of State and so-cial entrepreneurs. (Yes, some of the participants were people in shirts and ties trying to pitch their ideas for sustainable building ma-terials, renewable energy, and other social development challenges.) The idea for this radically different event, which we called Pitch & Flow, emerged after we had attended a social development goals (SDG) conference designed to connect social entrepreneurs with in-vestment.[19] Hour after hour at the SDG conference, well-meaning and well-dressed entrepreneurs presented their business plans to various judges and investors, hoping to secure funding for their visions of how to solve critical problems in the world. But by the end of the day, and after an overwhelming number of PowerPoint presentations, most of the entrepreneurs left empty-handed. Why had the entrepreneurs failed to win funding for their proposals? Certainly there wasn't a vision problem. These entrepreneurs had grand visions about how to solve some of society's biggest problems. But the visions weren't enough; the entrepreneurs needed something else.

In addition to a vision, they needed a story. Curiously, every entrepreneur presenting thought he or she had told a story. Each presenter described the problem observed, the envisioned solution, and how—with just a little funding—the entrepreneur could have a huge impact. But the presenters were still missing something. They were falling prey to something the corporate world has done for decades: using the word *story*, but really meaning *chronology* or *justification*. They were missing what makes a true narrative: a story with a narrative arc, characters, a conflict, and a resolution.

To solve the problem and teach the entrepreneurs to tell better stories, we wondered, why not pair the entrepreneurs with some of the world's best storytellers? Rappers! We collaborated with an eclectic mix of artists and change makers to create Pitch & Flow, the world's first rap battle, in partnership with the startup growth accelerator, Unreasonable Group, and the US Department of State, to address social development goals. Rappers like Doug E. Fresh, Young Paris, and Stretch Armstrong took the stage to tell why we should care about fair-trade apparel or re-offenses by convicted criminals. Social entrepreneur Samir Ibrahim and rapper Professor Lyrical won the rap battle for their project helping farmers in East Africa develop irrigation solutions with solar power. Artist Wes Felton's rap about the millions of people without electrical power was inspiring. Anyone who listens to it wants to change the world. As a result, for weeks afterward, Twitter was buzzing with people talking about social development goals that they were previously unaware of (for links to some of these pitches, see

"Digital Toolbox: Examples of Narratives Told Well—Rap Battles and Comics").

Why did Pitch & Flow work whereas impassioned PowerPoint presentations didn't? How did Pitch & Flow get the United Nations, the State Department, rappers, and social entrepreneurs to work together? The answer: strategic narrative. *Narrative* is another word for *story*, but we use it here to differentiate a bit from the overused word *story* and to emphasize something that has a narrative arc (character, dilemmas, and resolution) that persuades us to take action. Narrative works, in part, because it helps us suspend our disbelief and because it creates emotion, belief, and change.

Neil Gaiman, a widely published author who has won the Hugo, Nebula, and Bram Stoker awards as well as the Newbery and Carnegie medals, argues that stories give us the beliefs and tools to create a better world. In a recent article, he recalled how his ninety-seven-year-old cousin Helen survived the Holocaust with storytelling. At the time, books were outlawed in the ghetto and the Nazis would execute anyone on sight caught with a book. Helen had been secretly teaching a group of twenty girls math, Polish, and grammar. Then one day, someone slipped Helen a Polish translation of *Gone with the Wind*. At night, Helen would black out the windows and stay up reading. Then, in the morning, she would tell the girls the story. When Gaiman asked, "Why would you risk death—for a story?" his cousin replied, "Because for an hour every day, those girls weren't in the ghetto—they were in the American South; they were having adventures; they got away." Looking back on that story, Gaiman concludes, "[Storytelling] can furnish you with armor, with knowledge, with weapons, with tools you can take back into your life to help make it better . . . It's a real escape—and when you come back, you come back better-armed than when you left. Helen's story is a true story, and this is what we learn from it—that stories are worth risking your life for; they're worth dying for."[20]

The transformation process uses stories because they motivate people. But in addition to motivating people, stories also act, at the neural level, to persuade. At the level of the brain, a story can persuade so deeply that it actually leads to synchronization between speaker and listener, increasing the likelihood that they see the world the same way. For example, in one famous experiment, neuroscientists Uri Hasson and colleagues asked people to watch the movie *The Good, the Bad, and the Ugly* while the researchers took magnetic resonance images (MRIs) of the viewers' brains. Hasson and his colleagues found that as people followed the story, their brains moved in sync, particularly around key elements of the story. This synchronization occurred across extensive areas of the brain, including the regions responsible for language, hearing, association, emotion, and empathy.[21]

But the results show that stories not only lead people's brains to fire in the same way, but also lead people to see the world in the same way, a process neuroscientists call *coupling*.[22] To illustrate, in a separate experiment, Hasson and colleagues at Princeton had participants listen to another student telling a story about her prom date (which involved scuba diving, romantic intrigue, a fight between competing lovers, a car wreck, police, and blood). The researchers observed that not only did the brains of the storyteller and listener sync, but they coupled such that the listener's brain activity actually preceded the storyteller's brain activity, anticipating and syncing with the storyteller's brain.[23] Thus, at a neural level, storytelling changes our brain activity to become more in sync.[24]

In addition to synching our brains, narrative can also play a crucial role in persuading others by changing our latent theories—the hidden, unobserved, and often-biased theories that influence our decision making. These theories, sometimes called folk theories, are typically oversimplified, unexamined, and often inaccurate views about how something works (e.g., business, products, and relationships).[25] For example, if you ask people if they know how a toilet works, on a scale from 1 to 10 (high), almost everyone will report 10—they know exactly how a toilet works. But if you ask those same people to draw a schematic of how a toilet actually works, almost no one can![26] Stories can be critical to reshaping the latent folk theories that stand in the way of transformation.

Consider the case of Intel's struggles to make the leap from desktop PC to mobile microprocessors. In the premobile, PC world, processor advancements had been measured in terms of processor frequency, which translated directly into profits. When Intel started to develop mobile chips, these new chips were lower frequency (though higher performance) to conserve the mobile battery's power. However, because these new, low-frequency chips violated some of the senior executives' folk theory about the microprocessor business model (higher frequency equals higher performance leading to higher profit), some of the executives were not supportive of the project and decided to kill it.

Fortunately for Intel, Shmuel "Mooly" Eden, senior vice president at Intel and president of Intel Israel, didn't give up. He decided to ignore the direct order and kept working on mobile chips in Israel. Later, after his group had made more progress, he returned to the executives with a story about buying a beautiful, fast new car. At the end of the story, he asked, Do you care about how many RPMs or the torque on the engine, or do you care about performance—how fast it goes (its velocity) and how it feels? He then argued that in the mobile chipset world, four new performance indicators (e.g., small form factor, low power consumption, connection to Wi-Fi, and heat dissipation)—not frequency—are what really contribute to performance. The story helped the executives reshape their folk theories about the relationship between frequency and profit. Their theories were changed sufficiently that the leaders then lent their support to the project, which ultimately led to the development of Centrino processors—one of Intel's most successful leaps across technology generations.[27]

In short, although narrative may sound like a soft and fuzzy idea, it is both one of our oldest persuasive tools and one with deep neural and psychological foundations. Narratives lead our brains to literally synchronize and reorganize to understand one another and cooperate together. In some ways, stories are among the first human innovations—our universal code. But we can't access the power of this technology when we tell chronologies of events or wrap a project in justifications and then label it a story. A story must have a narrative arc to have impact; it needs characters, a conflict, and a resolution. In Ellen Langer's experiment, the researchers couldn't just tell the older men to think of themselves as younger. It was the narrative they lived in that changed how the men thought about themselves, at a deeply subconscious level, literally turning back the clock in their minds and bodies.

How to Use Strategic Narrative

When using narrative, your goal is to develop story arcs containing characters, conflict, and resolution that create a reason to believe for the listeners.

1. *Determine the characters.* Narratives always build around a protagonist, the central actor. In our stories, the customer or user is usually the central actor.

    • Write a story that has characters. In our research using applied neuroscience, we found that stories with characters with whom readers could identify just a little bit had a 35 percent higher impact on the persuasive ability of the narrative than did stories without such characters. For a dramatic illustration of the importance of using real people in storytelling, see the sidebar "Great Stories Are Told through the Eyes of One Person."

    • Consider other relevant actors, for example, economic users (the ones who pay for the product or service), technical users (who install and support the product or service), and antagonists (who might oppose the product or service).

2. *Build the narrative arc around the conflict.* All good narratives have a conflict—something that the character struggles to do. The conflict should be at the center of the story.

- Build conflicts around the customer job to be done—the underlying task for which people are actually hiring products. For example, customers don't come to Lowe's stores because they inherently want to buy new cabinets and sinks. They come because their job to be done is the creation of a beautiful place to live. So when we shaped stories about people using mixed reality to remodel their homes, we focused on the struggle to envision this beautiful place and to communicate the vision. For example, we did not focus on how they could use the stores better; the job to be done is not buying things at stores, but creating a beautiful remodel.

- Remember that all jobs to be done have emotional components (how does it make me feel?) and social components (how does it make me look?), not just functional components (what does it do?). Build stories around all three elements. For example, when we built the mixed-reality story, the characters struggled not only with what to choose but also with the difficult emotions involved in choosing.

- Do not build the story around your technology or products and services. Your products and services are not the conflicts. They are only a means to resolving the conflict. The characters and conflict remain at the center of the story.

3. *Define a resolution.* The resolution contains your vision for the transformational leap that allows you to solve the problem.

- Include your technology, products, or services as part of the vision for how to resolve the conflict.

- Think broadly about how to resolve the conflict (rather than narrowly on one specific solution) since your vision may evolve. For example, in the mixed-reality story, we left room for VR and AR solutions and then experimented with both.

- Include a hero. Customers and employees love to be the heroes who resolve the problem or who use the technology to be heroes.

Caveats and Alternatives: Pay Attention to the Folk Theory

As you develop your stories, you may need to pause and think about the underlying folk theories that guide your organization. If you are going to violate one of these theories, your story must (1) address why you will violate the theory and (2) provide a compelling, believable alternative. For example, in the Centrino example, Eden told a story that called Intel's existing folk theory into question. He then provided company executives with an alternate folk theory (the four new performance dimensions that matter in a mobile processing world). Alternatively, if you can build a story that works with your organization's existing folk theory, you will have an easier time communicating and gaining support for your narrative. For example, in the Lowe's AR and VR story, the company already believed in helping customers envision remodels using in-store displays and consultants. Mixed reality fit easily into its folk theory of how the world works.

Master Class: The Dangers of Setting and Revising Expectations with Narratives

Although narratives have incredible power to help others to believe in the future, they also involve trade-offs. In their review of the research on using stories to gain support, Raghu Garud, Henri

Great Stories Are Told through the Eyes of One Person

Some years ago, Leslie Norris, widely considered one of the most important Welsh authors and poets of the postwar period, taught us a critical lesson about telling great stories. "You can never tell a tragedy in generalities," he said. "You must always tell it through the story of one person." To illustrate, Norris told about the Aberfan disaster, in which a mountain of mining slag in Aberfan, Wales, slid down the hillside and killed many of the people in the town. He then paused and asked, "What do you feel?" We didn't feel much at the moment. Most likely, neither do you, or at most you may feel a modest sadness for the tragedy.

Then Norris taught us his most powerful lesson. He said, "Now let me tell you the story again." He told about being a small boy and having the great rugby champion David Beynon as his teacher. He told about his memories of Beynon, of his incredible size compared to the boys, whose feet sometimes didn't touch the floor when sitting in his chairs. Norris described Beynon's strength, and how when playing rugby he could run with six boys clinging to him as he laughed to score at the touch line. Then Norris told how, years later, he heard the news of the Aberfan disaster. He described how when the great mountain of slag came crashing down on the small town, the hysterical rescuers had raced to the scene. They started first at the elementary school, digging frantically. When at last they found Beynon's body, they found him with his great arms stretched out to protect the bodies of the small boys.

Norris paused. Forty years later, even after telling the story many times and writing one of his most famous poems on the subject, he had to pause to compose himself.[28] Then he asked, in his slow, lilting Welsh accent, "Now, what do you feel?" In that moment, Norris taught us the most powerful lesson we could share about telling stories. Stories are told through the lens of one person, their struggles, their lives, and their emotions. Similarly, great stories are made of specifics, details like the time, the place, the feel, and the smells. Use these particulars to construct motivating stories.

TABLE 2-1

How narratives create beliefs and expectations

	Believable	Expectations
Plot	Provides vivid but plausible vision of a possible future	Defines beneficial end state and the steps leading to the desired outcome
	Example: "One day, you won't need a car. Uber will deliver everything you need wherever and whenever you need it."	Example: "In a year, this will be worth ten times what it's worth now."
Connections	Creates links to broader forces (trends, successes, analogies, prestigious actors, etc.)	Creates links to growth expectations and the benefits within a field or an industry
	Examples: "The Airbnb of warehouses," "Google has invested in us"	Example: "In the new economy, firstcomer will be the winner-takes-all"

Source: Adapted from Raghu Garud, Henri A. Schildt, and Theresa K. Lant, "Entrepreneurial Story-telling, Future Expectations, and the Paradox of Legitimacy," *Organization Science* 25, no. 5 (2014): 1479–1492.

Schildt, and Theresa Lant argued that stories both help others believe in a possible future and set expectations.[29] Stories do this through the plot and by drawing connections to other external trends, such as successful companies (e.g., "we are going to be the Amazon of . . .") or prominent individuals (table 2-1).

Garud and his colleagues suggest two key points for master storytellers. First, be careful about setting expectations: although high expectations for success and profits may help you win short-term support, paradoxically they can create long-term challenges in fulfilling those expectations, leading to the loss of belief in your efforts. Furthermore, no plan survives first contact with reality, so the one thing we can guarantee is that reality will prove different from your vision for it. Thus, build room in your narrative for pivoting, or changing.

Second, there is a trade-off between believability and expectations: providing more-specific details in an effort to create a believable plot can lower the audience's expectations that it will succeed

Examples of Narratives Told Well— Rap Battles and Comics

If you go online you can find examples of songs from the Pitch & Flow rap battle (yes, it really happened, go read about it in *XXL* Magazine or *Vibe*) and example comics (discussed in the next section).[30] For more information, see our website: leadingtransformationbook.com.

(people start to see all the hurdles in getting to the end goal), whereas setting overly high expectations can decrease the believability of the story. Research suggests that to hit the optimal balance between believability and expectations, you should match the level of abstraction in your story to the timing of your story. The further in the future your story occurs, the better more abstract stories work, creating commitment rather than critical evaluation.[31] How do you increase the level of abstraction? Use more analogies and metaphors. These more abstract story tools allow flexibility in interpretation by the audience and create credibility for the story.[32] In chapter 4, we describe what to do when something goes not as expected and you have to change your story.

Tool: Comic Books

Once you have envisioned a valuable new future and developed a strategic narrative to persuade others, you still need to find a way to communicate the vision and story. Our favorite medium is a comic book, or graphic novel. We recognize that for a world where most organizations spend weeks honing their PowerPoint presentations to have maximum impact, the idea of a comic book sounds ludicrous.

Imagine Kyle's trepidation when he first gave a comic book to his executive leadership team. We aren't minimizing that a comic book is a bit unconventional. But we have conducted several neuroscience studies to understand which medium—PowerPoint, talking, video, or comics—has the most persuasive power for convincing others to follow a grand vision. When we observe people's actual neural reactions using objective measures (explained later), which are much more accurate indicators than what they say, we discover the power of the graphic novel. Comic books generate a great deal of positive emotional response and the most optimal cognitive load. They generate the most engagement and lead to the most appropriate emotional reactions (e.g., people respond positively to the positive parts of the story, and vice versa). Finally, comic books produce the strongest recall (including people's recall of episodes in the narrative and the key elements in the story). Why, then, does something so unusual work so well?

Comic books work well to tell the story, precisely because they are different. Most organizations live in a state of PowerPoint saturation. As a result, when we sit in yet another PowerPoint presentation, most of us go into a subconscious frame of reference focused on taking in and evaluating information. A graphic novel breaks this cognitive frame by providing a new format that leads us to shift from a critical evaluation of incremental details to the suspension of disbelief long enough to entertain a new idea. The medium also works because the images create a second channel of communication—visual communication—that reinforces the story but also constrains it since the narrative must become very focused and tight to fit into a graphic novel format. Finally, comics work because we expect them, as a format, to convey a vision of the future, and we are more accepting of this vision because of that expectation.

Of course, you can use other formats to tell your story, and they can be equally successful. For example, years ago, Børge Mogensen, one of the architects of the Danish Modern movement, in an effort to change how people thought about furniture, created hilarious films in which workers stormed a Danish home full of heavy, over-bearing furniture; they then took the furniture out back and exe-cuted it by firing squad. They replaced it with new furniture, using honest materials that could be repurposed for the modern lifestyle and that emphasized function as well as form. Today, many attri-bute the movement's success to the efforts of Mogensen, architect Kaare Klint, the furniture makers, and others to tell interconnected stories that led to Danish Modern movement's becoming an inter-national sensation that still shapes design today.[33]

How to Use Comics (and Related Tools)

Despite comic books' unconventional way of sharing a view of the future in a business environment, we nevertheless recommend spe-cific steps for making sure this medium succeeds.

1. *Define the format.* Identify the medium, the creative compo-nents, and the artistic capabilities (e.g., which artists) you need to communicate the narrative (see the sidebar "How to Find and Evaluate Graphic Artists" for details on selecting the right talent).

   - Explore the right format for your organization whether that be comics, video, inspirational speech, PowerPoint, rap battle, etc. To do this, ask yourself, what is my premise—my foundational assumption—about how to have an impact and then choose a medium that makes your content come alive.

   - Don't be fooled into thinking PowerPoint is creative—it is a rectangle with more rectangles inside it. So find some-thing more creative if you are going to use this familiar tool, otherwise you will have an uphill battle.

   - Strike a balance between novel and insincere, "cheesy," or uncomfortable.

How to Find and Evaluate Graphic Artists

How can you find graphic artist to create your comics? One of the best places to look is the local comic cons (comic conventions). Avoid the big Comic-Con, which is more of a party. By contrast, the local comic cons are more like job fairs, with artists exhibiting their work and looking for more work. You can literally walk around and look for artists who have a style you are looking for. If you can't attend the event, you can look at the list of exhibitors, most of whom have art posted online. Alternatively, you can explore colleges, art schools, or the work of freelance graphic artists. For example, in the past we have taught a class at the Savannah College of Art and Design.

You are looking for artists whose drawing you like, but who aren't too over-the-top. In addition, it helps to have someone who has colored or inked for a major magazine (which shows that the person has quite a bit of talent) but who isn't a regular contributor (such an artist might be more available—and willing—to work). Then as you start to work with an artist, keep in mind that you are looking for someone who can receive feedback and maybe even give a little feedback to you. For example, the person may say to you, "I heard you that you wanted X, but you might also think about this." The artists who are both receptive to feedback and proactive are worth their weight in gold.

When it comes time to contract the artists, the same rules apply to the artists as to the writers. As you test out both artists and writers, remember that this is a creative process and sometimes it just doesn't work as expected and you need to start over. Don't be afraid to pivot or restart.

2. *Shape the artist.* Have the artist focus on the most important part of the narrative, including your solution.

- Push the artist to focus on your technology or solution in a natural way. Otherwise, artists tend to get carried away by the technology itself.

- Do not overcomplicate the narrative or the visuals. Overly complex elements will decrease the impact on readers.

3. *Iterate the testing of the comic book.* Test and retest the comic with your audiences to discover and then pivot on areas that do not resonate.

- Pay attention to body language when people read the comic: are people stalling, looking away, leaning back in the chair, crossing arms, laughing, or snickering?

- Ask people what they recall from the story, what resonated, and what didn't work, and then iterate this process. We iterate sometimes ten times on a comic.

- Test using all your available tools. We neuroprototype the comics using applied neuroscience tools (described later) to see precisely where the story resonates or where it

DIGITAL TOOLBOX

Finding Graphic Artists and Contracting Them

Online, we provide links to sample contracts you can use with graphic artists. Our website, leadingtransformationbook.com, can also connect you to certified graphic artists whom we have worked with or who attended a course we have taught. You can also try online platforms that can connect you to creative talent (e.g., Fiverr.com).

overwhelms the reader. But even if you don't have access to these tools, you can use other feedback tools or some tools from "Digital Toolbox: Assessing Comics" to get some indicators whether you are heading in the right direction.

Caveats and Alternatives: When Comics Don't Work

Recently, an executive approached us at a conference. He leaned close and in an aggressive tone said, "I tried your comic thing, and it didn't work."

We know we don't have all the answers and that one solution does not fit all. But we were curious and asked to hear more.

"Well," he said, "I hired a graphic artist, and he put our strategy into a comic book, and it didn't make any difference. People thought it was stupid."

We then asked if he had used a tool, like science fiction, to develop a vision of the future.

"Not really," he said. "It was just our current strategy."

Then we asked if he had created a strategic narrative, with characters, conflict, and resolution.

"Well, no, you can't really do that with our strategy."

We asked about the other parts of the process. Had he followed any of our recommendations? No. He had just taken the comic and tried to apply it as a stand-alone tool. We tried to explain that just lifting comics out of the process is a bit like taking the fuel system out of a car and then expecting to drive to Los Angeles. The tools are part of an interrelated set of activities—none of them is magic alone (what we call sufficient in philosophy).

Nor do comic books work when you try to show them to people who dislike comics, but when you have not first framed the problem you are trying to solve. (In fact, somewhat secretly, not all the authors of the book are fans of comics in the broader world.) Some people will struggle with your medium (i.e., the graphic novel) or your story. You can help the situation by clarifying why you are doing it, to help people get over their initial social discomfort at something like a comic.

We find that the following steps help. First, acknowledge the situation honestly and perhaps with a touch of humor: "We can all admit that comics are a bit weird, but if we really want to do things in new ways, perhaps we should try something new." Second, reframe the meeting where you introduce the comics around the common problem. For example, "We all recognize that our industry is changing quickly and we keep getting stuck in incremental initiatives. The challenge is to think bigger and bolder. To help us do that, we are going to try something totally different to help us see things in a new way: a story, told in this case with a comic book." Third, seek common ground with the resistors. Find out what their concerns are, and speak to those concerns. Fourth, if possible, have a prestigious individual—an internal leader or an influencer—speak up about the ways in which he or she thinks using comics (or your chosen medium) to convey the vision is a good idea. Enlisting the backing of someone with cachet can help win support from others.

Master Class: How to Get Users to Accept Something Really Outlandish

Can you get people to eat bugs? Although that might sound like an esoteric question, it's representative of a larger problem studied by Spencer Harrison and his colleagues about how to persuade people to accept radical new things. Harrison started by trying to understand how companies creating food out of insects overcame the natural tendency of consumers to reject something counter to the status quo. In his research on insect companies and other radical innovations like houses made from mushrooms and toilets with augers, Harrison found that to win acceptance for radically different

Assessing Comics

As we describe in chapter 4, you should test your stories and comics using experimental design. Some of the best tools are those derived from applied neuroscience (see chapter 4 for a full description). One shortcut tool that you can try is an online assessment tool called Neurovision, created by Thomas, our neuroscientist coauthor. The tool lets you feed in a scan of your image, comic, or PowerPoint, page by page, and have it analyzed. Using one of the largest behavioral databases in the world, the tool then scores the image according to the complexity of the work (on a scale of 0 to 100 percent) and identifies the areas of the image that will generate attention from viewers.

The optimal level of complexity depends on your desired goal. For example, when you walk into a store selling Lego toys, the store would like the level of complexity to be high and visual attention to be dispersed because Lego wants to create the "wall of Lego" effect, or the sense that there are almost infinite choices with Lego. By contrast, an online services provider wants complexity to be low and visual attention to be focused when trying to convert site visitors to paid subscriptions. For comics, the optimal level of complexity is below 55 percent, the point at which positive emotion turns neutral and, later, negative. At lower complexity scores, such as 20 percent, motivation can be very positive and associated with wanting. Furthermore, you want visual attention focused on the key elements of the narrative and your solution, not on random details. You can find more details on our website, leadingtransformationbook.com.

ideas, you need to amp up either the novelty or the usefulness while downplaying the other element.[34]

Specifically, Harrison's group noted that some inventors won acceptance for their radical ideas by stressing the novelty of the idea while downplaying its usefulness. For example, they emphasized the novelty of putting a scorpion in a lollipop or creating a roulette game where you win chocolates, some of which contain nuts and the others, grasshoppers. Each inventor touted the novelty over the usefulness. Although the idea of scorpion or grasshopper candy sounds kooky, these entrepreneurs were more successful at winning acceptance for their radical ideas by promoting the novelty of the treats than the inventors would have been if they had plugged the treats' usefulness.

Alternatively, other inventors in Harrison's study won acceptance for their radical ideas by stressing usefulness over novelty. For example, in the bugs-as-food world, one company marketed its product as sustainable, gluten-free flour that is a one-for-one substitute for real flour, downplaying the product's unconventional source. Another inventor developed a process to make T-shirts from the cellulose in cow manure. But to win acceptance, the inventor found she had to emphasize the process's usefulness as a carbon-capture tool (cellulose is incredibly difficult to break down and reuse after it has passed through the various parts of a cow's stomach).[35]

A final technique is to put the radical idea in a format others already accept. For example, when Thomas Edison tried to commercialize the light bulb, he experimented endlessly to dim the light generated from the bulb. Why? He wanted the light output to match that of existing gaslights. He also designed a distributed electricity system so that he could approach prospective customers and explain that it works just like gas lighting—it produces the same amount of light, the wires go in the same pipes as for gas lighting, but it is cleaner and more reliable.[36]

Summary

In closing, we introduced the idea that transformation begins by setting the vision and the direction you should be heading, the specific vector of search. We acknowledged the primary behavioral limitation, namely, the tendency to be trapped by incrementalism. To address this behavioral challenge, we introduced a set of tools, starting with *science fiction*, or speculative organizational fiction, as a mechanism to dream bigger and envision other valuable, possible futures. We then talked about describing this potential future using a *strategic narrative* that has a dramatic arc, including characters and conflict, to give people a reason to believe. Finally, we talked about tools to convey the story, hopefully in a meaningful and compelling way, such as in *comic books*.

Ultimately, our goal has been to break the tendency to be incremental. If you find that other tools help your organization break this habit better, then please use them. But don't forget the power of imagination encapsulated in a true narrative. Stories are some of our oldest tools, and they may ultimately be some of our most important tools to taking charge of our future.

THREE

Breaking Bottlenecks

Using Decision Maps and Archetypes

In his book on habits, Charles Duhigg recalls a now-famous speech Paul O'Neill gave to investors when he took over as CEO of the multibillion-dollar metals company Alcoa. The company, which makes the aluminum that goes into Coke cans and Hershey Kisses wrappers, among other products, had been struggling for some time while competitors stole away market share. Several new product lines had failed. Fifteen thousand workers had recently gone on strike, and the unions were angrily gearing up for another fight with the new CEO, who would surely focus on cutting more costs to fix the declining margins.

When O'Neill stepped to the podium for his first speech as CEO on an October day in New York City, the room was tense. Investors and analysts waited nervously, anxious to hear how the new CEO would fix Alcoa's flagging profitability. But when O'Neill started talking, he didn't mention revenue, costs, or profits. He didn't mention the strikes. He didn't talk about how he would fix the inventory problems or competitors stealing market share. Instead, he began by saying, "I want to talk to you about worker safety."[1]

The stunned room went silent.

As O'Neill started to elaborate on the dangers workers face, a few investors turned to look at each other quizzically. O'Neill persisted: "Our employees work with metals that are 1,500 degrees and machines that can rip a man's arm off."[2] He continued, talking about how he would make safety his number one priority. At the end of the strange speech, one of the investors asked about capital ratios. Another investor asked about excess inventory in the aerospace division. O'Neill responded, "I'm not certain you heard me . . . if you want to understand how Alcoa is doing, you need to look at our workplace safety figures."

As soon as questions ended, the shocked investors rushed to the doors. One broker said he actually ran from the room to get on the phone, telling his twenty largest clients to sell their stock: "The board put a crazy hippie in charge, and he's going to kill the company." He now admits it was the worst advice he ever gave. Within a year, profits had hit record levels. By the end of O'Neill's tenure, the value of an Alcoa investment was impressive: if you had invested $1 million in Alcoa the day O'Neill joined, by the time he left, you would have received another million in dividends, and your stock would have been worth $5 million.

What's puzzling about the return on investment is why it would be so high when O'Neill seemed to be attacking something so peripheral to performance: safety. But O'Neill's strategy was brilliant because it attacked the core behavioral bottleneck in the company—its habits and routines—in the language it understood and could accept (taking care of the workers). Alcoa had historically been more of a caretaker organization (see the later section "Tool: Organizational Nomenclature"). It took good care of its workers but, along the way, had developed inefficient processes, waste, and high labor costs. Trying to change these directly by demanding cost cuts, better margins, or labor reductions would be a challenge to the company's core identity of taking care of its workers. Thus, a direct attack on these values would be like running a battering ram against the castle gate—it would bring the entire organization, tasked with taking care of the people inside the company, out to the proverbial walls to defend it.

Instead of attacking these cherished values, O'Neill subtly spoke in the language—or nomenclature—of these values, emphasizing the importance of safety in taking care of the employees, allowing them to accept the initiative he proposed, precisely because it matched their values. It was a stroke of genius because the safety effort itself was a Trojan horse to discovering and correcting massive inefficiencies that had built up over time. Later, reflecting on his experience, O'Neill describes his intent very clearly: "I knew I had to transform Alcoa. But you can't order people to change. So I decided I was going to start by focusing on one thing. If I could start disrupting the habits around one thing, it would spread throughout the entire company." O'Neill's story illustrates a master stroke in transformational change because it uses a behavioral solution to a primary bottleneck in innovation and change—people's habits. This chapter describes how you can use behavioral solutions to identify and break similar roadblocks to change in your situation.

The Need: New Tools to Break through Habit and Routine

From the street, the Neurons Building, Thomas's headquarters, has an impressive eighteenth-century Danish building style. Largely brick, the building is part of an old military barracks where cannons and shells were once manufactured for European wars. But today the barracks hold racks of high-resolution EEG headsets, eye trackers, and servers crunching behavioral data. As one of the leading scientists at the intersection of psychology, neuroscience, and economics, Thomas has already done some of foundational research that helps explain how the brain drives our decisions.

For example, prior theories of the conscious and subconscious mind argued that consciousness operates like a light switch, either on or off. But one evening, as Thomas was reading the writings of the nineteenth-century psychologist William James, he was struck by a passage. James described the peculiar state of consciousness when you try to recall a forgotten name—a state in which there is a gap between remembering and not remembering. Thomas began to wonder, could the dominant view of consciousness be wrong? Could consciousness exist in a halfway state, neither fully conscious nor completely subconscious, and could such a state lead to this gap that James describes?

To test the theory, Thomas designed a series of experiments using functional magnetic resonance imaging (fMRI) brain scanning. In the experiments, Thomas and his coauthors flashed images past people and then examined the participants' brain responses when they reported being aware, not aware, or partly aware of the image. The team found that, counter to the dominant view, consciousness is not an on-off switch, but rather a continuous process that involves the gradual engagement of different brain regions.[3] More important, they found that the transition of a process to consciousness requires the engagement of massive brain resources and expansive regions of the brain.[4] This huge global brain mobilization helps explain why we so often fall into biases in our thinking. The brain, in an effort to conserve energy, relies on intuition, subconscious feelings, and routines whenever it can, and this reliance often leads to very biased thinking.

Prior research has overwhelmingly shown the dangers of relying on this intuitive, habitual system. This system of thinking, labeled *system 1 thinking* by Keith Stanovich and Richard West, was popularized by Nobel Prize–winning psychologist Daniel Kahneman. System 1 thinking, which is intuitive and subconscious, while quick and efficient, also regularly leads us to make mistakes in calculation, judgment, decision making, and other important activities.[5] To illustrate the power of these intuitive, routine, but unexamined judgments, in one experiment, a confederate (someone part of the team running the experiment) tried to cut in the line for a busy copy machine. If the confederate provided an unqualified reason (e.g., "Excuse me, may I use the Xerox machine?"), people in line said no. But if the confederate provided any kind of explanation, even the most silly (e.g., "Excuse me, may I use the Xerox machine *because I want to make copies?*"), people let the confederate skip the line. Why? Because their intuitive system of thinking is preprogramed to accept explanations for actions without challenging them, even when the reasons are completely illogical.[6] Similarly, when tested, people almost always give the wrong answer to a simple mathematics question: "A bat and a ball cost $1.10. The bat costs $1.00 more than the ball. How much does the ball cost?" Most people answer $0.10 even though the correct answer is $0.05. Why? Because intuitively $0.10 is one dollar less than the total, and our brains land quickly on the intuitive answer. To think through the problem properly requires some thought, and we must recognize that if the ball costs $0.10 then the bat would cost $1.10, for a total of $1.20, which is more than the total in the question.[7] These, and hundreds of other clever experiments, demonstrate the pervasiveness and power of the intuitive mental processes that reinforce habit and that can bias many of the decisions in our lives.

Of course, routines in and of themselves aren't evil. They are created to save time and energy. But we rarely reexamine them, because once they have become so ingrained in our behavior, reexamination is costly. In fact, Thomas once explained to his students that bike riding habits are so ingrained that if you focus too much on turning the pedals, you can actually disable your system 1 thinking (habit) as system 2 thinking (analysis) starts to compete with it. The next day, one of his students came in with scabs on his palms and a bruise on his elbow. He explained, "I went ahead and tried it—paying attention to turning the pedals—and I fell off my bike!"

To make matters worse, the areas of the habitual system 1 thinking have a diabolic dual property that make changing habits even more difficult. Brain regions with obnoxiously difficult names such as the globus pallidus, putamen, and ventral striatum are deeply situated and not accessible through conscious thought or control. This means that we can never directly control our habits but must instead resort to indirect means. Furthermore, the same brain network has a more or less direct connection to the body's movements, and thus the decisions occurring at this subcortical and subconscious level have a more direct route to action, sometimes circumventing willpower. Breaking habits requires either overcoming both the speed of subconscious choice and the lack of direct access to these processes, or another more subtle approach, like the one O'Neill used when transforming Alcoa.

The Process: How to Break Bottlenecks Using Decision Maps and Archetypes

Recently we worked with a major wholesale distributor of industrial parts (we've disguised the company and technology to comply with a nondisclosure agreement). One of the major problems for a distributor is the complexity of stocking and distributing hundreds of thousands of items. The company we worked with got a head start by using the process we described in chapter 2. The wholesaler used science fiction to envision a future in which drones would help workers keep track of inventory and deliver it for packing. Using the tools described in chapter 2, the wholesaler created a compelling narrative and then told the story using a comic book.

Despite the power of the narrative to encourage people to believe, there was still a great deal of work to get everyone mentally and emotionally behind the idea of drones in a closed environment with people. Although drones doing inventory may not sound so radical today, it wasn't so obvious just a few years ago. For a moment, imagine the risks of being the first wholesaler to put drones into warehouses. What would happen if the drone injured someone, leading to multimillion-dollar settlements and a barrage of negative press? How would staff react to the idea of drones in warehouses potentially threatening their jobs? What would happen if the drone took incorrect inventory of a mission-critical part, causing unacceptable delays for an important customer?

Although our prior work gave the wholesaler some confidence that the transformation process could work, the hurdles for getting people on board with drones in warehouses created a major bottleneck. Resistance started to pop up from every corner, and for good reason. Routines established to protect the company from risks and uncertainty were being activated, threatening to stop the project before it even got off the ground. How, then, did the wholesaler move past these hurdles?

Before we created the narrative and the comic book, we spent some time conducting in-depth interviews. These interviews helped us understand the *organizational nomenclature*, or the type of organization and the language in which people talk about what they value and do. This understanding helped us to frame the narrative in the organization's value language so that people could understand it more easily. We also created a *decision map* of the formal and informal decision structure inside the company. Thus, we had a sense of who sat in the key decision-making roles, especially the hierarchy not on the org chart. Moreover, we analyzed what made these people tick or, more accurately, what made them tick in their role in the organization and how they responded in that role to new things, called their *functional archetype* (which we will explain later in this chapter). This chapter is organized around the three action steps just described: (1) translate your ideas into the language that your organization speaks; (2) map how decisions are made to focus your efforts on those who matter most; and (3) understand what motivates these key decision makers, and orient your pitches to align with those drivers.

As we sized up the resistance to the drones project, we knew that, despite many potential bottlenecks, we had two priority questions to answer. First, who needs to say yes to get this project into warehouses? Second, how much effort should be expended to get a yes? (You can spend all your effort to win a battle, but still lose a war.) We could see that many key decision makers wanted proof that the drones were safe in the warehouses before authorizing them. But how could we prove that they were safe if we couldn't get permission to get them in warehouses in the first place? Fortunately, one decision maker in our map was different—the CEO of a recent acquisition running a smaller network of the distribution center. Not only did he have full authority to put the drones in warehouses, but he was also wired a bit differently. He was more of a maverick. When we approached him with the comic book and shared the vision, he grasped it immediately and authorized an initial proof of concept. Breaking this small bottleneck to find an initial launchpoint for the project was the first step toward breaking the bottleneck in the rest of the organization.

Next, we had to figure out how to make the drones, since distributors have not historically been leaders in new technology. We visited every major drone company in North America and Asia. Most companies were so interested in their own projects that no one wanted to take on the project of a paying customer that differed from their own vision. In a classic innovation trap, the firms were so busy creating the solutions they thought customers wanted that they didn't pay attention to what an actual customer—a major company—wanted to pay them to build. Thus, to get started building drones, the company had to find an uncommon partner, the kind of partner you don't normally work with and that brings complementary capabilities to help you make a long leap. We found our uncommon partner, a startup working out of a poorly ventilated office space in Silicon Valley.

Before we arrived, the startup had been building high-power consumer drones, an effort that looked like an increasingly hopeless effort in the face of major competitors like DJI. But unlike their colleagues at larger companies, when we showed the comic book to the startup and told them we wanted to partner on commercial drones for distributors, they listened. They were willing to build on the concepts we had introduced in the story. Nine months later, the warehouse drone (WD-1) was flying around warehouses, reading RFID tags, scanning labels, and taking inventory for organized parts (parts that had been broken down out of their larger supply boxes into marked containers). Moreover, workers in the warehouse found that the drones saved them from the tiresome and frustrating task of continuously taking inventory, allowing them to focus on other, often more important tasks they had been putting off.

The speed with which we had made the narrative real, and our early success with the prototype drone, WD-1, enabled us to break a bigger, organization-wide bottleneck. During a trip to Silicon Valley, the executive leadership team visited several tech giants and then came together in a small auditorium at Singularity University (SU)—the Silicon Valley think tank and business incubator—to review the progress on their different innovation projects, including the drone project. SU had long been an important catalyst for many companies, helping them envision how the world is changing. The room was buzzing with energy after the recent visit to Google, just down the road in Mountain View. Everything seemed calm and relaxed on the front stage. But backstage, it was panic and terror. After staying up for two nights in a row, the startup team was desperately patching together the more advanced drone prototype, the WD-2 (capable of taking inventory with both parts broken down into clearly marked bins, assessing bulk packaged parts, and inventorying parts stored on both floor- and storage-shelf levels). At the last minute, the build team was literally duct-taping the drone together while the engineers double-checked the programming. Then, with a half-hearted thumbs-up, they signaled that the drone was ready to go, and the presentation started.

Most of the presentation summarized the progress of various incremental initiatives inside the company. When the time to present the drones project came up, the project's head, Doug, stepped up and described WD-1's early success. He presented the initial results, and the other executives began to sit up in their seats and ask questions about its limitations. Always the showman, Doug stopped the questions, saying: "Before we get too far, let me show you the next generation of what we are working on: the WD-2!" The curtains parted, and with a buzz, the drone whirred onto the stage. Doug described how the drone could read both unpacked floor-level inventory in bins and bulk-packed inventory on upper-level storage shelves with a high level of accuracy. The new drone would create radical savings in inventory accuracy and at an incredibly low investment relative to the savings. Moreover, it had multiple redundant systems to make it safe. The room went silent for a full five seconds. Then it exploded with enthusiasm. "Holy smokes," "This is amazing," "How did you do this?" "How does it work?" One executive shouted out, "Why don't we have this already?" From his chair, the CEO from the recent acquisition, the one who had initially authorized testing the WD-1, turned around, smiling, and defended the decision vigorously: "Because you didn't want it? Remember?" Everyone laughed. The executive smiled back, "OK, well, I want it now!"

In that moment, with the proof on the table, the barriers big and small began to fall. Everyone was ready to put the drones in warehouses, and the project proceeded with few hang-ups thereafter. Although getting the commitment of the entire executive team may have seemed like haphazard good luck, it actually came about because we followed a very specific process designed to overcome the behavioral obstacles that distort and block decisions and action. The process involves applying the following four tools that help you get past these obstacles inside your organization.

Tool: Organizational Nomenclature

What kind of organization are you? This simple question can be surprisingly hard to answer and incredibly revealing. We recently sat down with a major apparel manufacturer, unrelated to Lowe's, that had been designing work clothing with technology elements such as fabric that can read gestures to advance a song being played or to provide nudges about the route to follow. The entire team was incredibly proud of the innovation. But initial feedback from users was mixed. Secretly, several team members started to become nervous about whether the new products would be a commercial success. Eventually, they called us in to help them assess their trajectory and see new possibilities.

Given all the talk about science fiction, they had expected us to show up with a quantum computer or neural-network artificial intelligence (AI) on a thumb drive. But the first thing we did was ask a simple question: "What kind of organization are you?" For a moment, the team around the table—senior vice presidents, head of design, head of innovation, and others—hesitated. Then debate ensued. Every comment had an underlying theme of design, but no one said it aloud until we asked, "Are you are a design company?" Everyone nodded. We then asked the follow-up question: "What does that mean about how you make decisions? About what you value?" Everyone agreed that the company valued . . . well, design—the aesthetics of new apparel, creating new designs, or updating current fashions. Finally, we challenged them: "As you think about this new technology-laced product line, what are customers looking for?" There was another moment of silence, and then looks of recognition spread across their faces. Then we asked, "Do you actually know what customers are looking for?"

Although the team had been building what felt like science fiction—work clothing that could give you directions or let you answer your phone without touching it—when we went out and asked workers what they wanted out of their clothing, they frequently expressed something very different. Most workers found the clothing they wore to work uncomfortable, not durable, and uninspiring. Workers really wanted something simpler—durable comfort with a bit of style.

But changing the views of the team at the clothing retailer wasn't as simple as returning and reporting that workers wanted something else. Initial conversations with some of the executives, led to typical responses like "They (meaning the customers) don't get it." Instead we had to recast the findings in the organization's nomenclature—design. We went back to the executives and spoke about the design needs of workers and the opportunity to create a new design category—the urban worker design inspired by skate culture. Both recasting the findings in a nomenclature the company could understand and the awareness the leadership team generated when we discussed with them how much they value design helped break down the bottlenecks to a major product reorientation. When we packaged the new insights correctly, the leadership team was able to accept them and get to work designing a new line of work clothing: one focused on comfort and durability on the inside with a bit of hipster and skater on the outside. The new look and the resulting clothing line has been an incredible success.

Thus, the first step in breaking organizational bottlenecks is to recognize the source of the bias so that you can face it head-on, in part, by using the organization's nomenclature, or the words that organization members use to reflect their values. If you try to persuade the members to see something new, but you are speaking a language they don't value or use, they won't hear you.

But as soon as you put the idea in terms they understand (e.g., designing comfortable clothing for workers), almost no matter how off-the-wall it may be, the idea suddenly becomes acceptable. One reason that O'Neill succeeded in transforming Alcoa was that he used organizational nomenclature (the focus on valuing workers) to address how to fix the company, rather than the aggressive

DIGITAL TOOLBOX

Determining Your Organization's Type

Sometimes it can be challenging to answer the question "What kind of organization are we?" from inside the organization. You might want to look at competitors or related companies and ask, "How do we compare with these players"? On our website, leadingtransformationbook .com, we suggest some tools and assessments that can help you get insight into your organization type to help you better identify the value language of the organization.

language of cost-cutting efficiency. Alternatively, an organization's nomenclature can reveal overlooked weaknesses that need to be addressed, as was the case for the clothing company we described. In many of the examples throughout the book, you will see the importance of this first tool: identifying and speaking the organization's language to break up decision bottlenecks. (See "Digital Toolbox: Determining Your Organization's Type" for more help on this challenge.)

How to Assess and Use the Nomenclature of the Organization

To use an organization's nomenclature, you need to identify the true focus of an organization by paying close attention to the everyday details of language: job titles, how people explain what they do, how presentations are created, and so forth. The sidebar "Tools to Assess Organizational Nomenclature" lays out in tabular form how you can organize your assessment.

1. *Define what the organization values.* Ask, "What kind of organization are we?"

- As you ask, "What kind of organization are we," ask your-self further clarifying questions such as: When making decisions, which arguments are valued? Who gets pro-moted, and for what? What do our presentations look like (high text or high graphics)? What is emphasized on the earnings call? How do we describe our own jobs? These questions reveal what the organization values. For example, look at the job titles at Microsoft and Adobe. Although the two companies made similar products for decades, the majority of job postings inside Microsoft were described as engineering roles, whereas inside Adobe, they were described as design roles.

2. *Speak in the organization's language.* Organizations respond to the language, values, and processes that match their arche-type. Speak in the value language—the values and words the organization uses—to break through to people inside the company.

   - Conduct in-depth interviews with key people in the organization. Have them tell you stories. Notice the words they use. For example, "charged the mountain" tells you something different from "made the customers happy." The stories they tell you also say a great deal about what they value and don't value.

   - Check your nomenclature with someone you trust, some-one who can give you honest feedback. For example, did you just use the name of a recently failed project?

In closing, use organizational nomenclature judiciously. Different groups inside, or outside, the organization may have different nomenclatures. Sometimes, the biggest source of resistance is sim-ply aligning the different languages and making the translation between groups.

Tools to Talk about Organizational Nomenclature

Sometimes it can be hard to get started recognizing your own nomenclature, from the inside. It may be helpful to think about the different types of organizations and how they value different things. For example, innovator and entrepreneur Andy Freire talks about five types of organizations and how they value different things (table 3-1).[a]

Alternatively, we sometimes say that organizations fall into different functional types, depending on what they do (table 3-2). Understanding what they value, or undervalue, can provide valuable insight into how to speak to the organization (what it values) or its blind spots (what it undervalues). You can often help the organization overcome its weaknesses by reframing the effort in terms of what the group undervalues (see the last column in table 3-2).

TABLE 3-1

Andy Freire's five organizational types

Organization types	Key values
Customer-centric	Customer focus and orientation
One team	Cooperation and oneness
Innovation	Learning and creation
Achievement	Getting things done
People first	Development and reward

Source: Summarized from Jeff McNeill, "5 Archetypes of Organizational Culture," McNeill.io, August 5, 2009, https://mcneill.io/5-archetypes-of-organizational-culture/.

a. Andrés "Andy" Freire, "Five Archetypes of Culture," video, *eCorner* (Stanford University newsletter), May 1, 2007, http://ecorner-legacy.stanford.edu/videos/1853/Five-Archetypes-of-Culture; *Wikipedia*, s.v. Andrés "Andy" Freire, last updated February 5, 2018, https://en.wikipedia.org/wiki/Andr%C3%A9s_Freire; Jeff McNeill, "5 Archetypes of Organizational Culture," *Mcneill.io* (blog), August 5, 2009, https://mcneill.io/5-archetypes-of-organizational-culture.

TABLE 3-2

Organization types (nonexhaustive)

Organization types	Examples	What the organization values	What it undervalues	How to communicate what it undervalues
Engineering	Google, Microsoft	Solutions, technology, sophistication	User needs	The highest-impact solutions start with user needs.
Cooperative	REI	Adventure, teamwork, equality	Individualism	The best way to advance our collective goals is through individual growth.
Disrupter	Tesla	Innovation, change, questioning	Status quo	We can apply lessons learned from the past to think differently about the future.
Social	United Nations	Humanity, access, global perspective	Traditional business thinking	By approaching our problems in a new way, can we achieve more success for humanitarian programs?

Tool: Decision Bottleneck Map

In 2017, one of the worst corporate security breaches exposed the personal financial information of millions of households in the United States and Europe. Ironically, although the security breach occurred via third-party software being used inside the company, the software vendor had released a patch to fix the breach the same day it was discovered. But almost four months later, Equifax still had not installed the patch, and the credit-reporting agency was hacked.

Why did it take so long to install a security patch? We can point the finger at Equifax, but we would be failing to see a bigger trend. As Mark Goodman, author of *Future Crimes*, argues, 95 percent of all cyber security issues are the result of human errors and problems, but only 1 percent of an organization's security budget focuses on these human factors, with the overwhelming majority of the spending dedicated to mostly ineffective technological "solutions." Goodman has argued that this very mismatch, between human behavior and technological solutionism, is at the heart of the exponential increase in cybercrime we are seeing around the world today.[8]

Then why did it take so long at Equifax to solve a simple problem? One answer has to do with how decisions are made inside most organizations, where information technology (IT) is seen as a support function or an afterthought rather than a core strategy function. Consequently, not just at Equifax, but at many companies, the investments, the hacks, and the security breaches really reflect how decisions are made.

As you think about your organization's decision making, ask yourself which office is the most powerful in your organization. Most people would say the corner office or where the CEO sits. But they would be missing something critical. Although the corner office may be where we put the person with the highest rank, it isn't necessarily where the most powerful person sits. Jeff Pfeffer, a Stanford professor and the author of several books on power in organizations, studied the question. He found that the most powerful locations in a workplace tended to be the offices near the bathroom and the watercooler. Why? Because the people in these offices can see everyone, speak to everyone, and know what is happening inside the organization. Although they may not be central in the formal hierarchy, their position at the center of the informal network provides them crucial information and power advantages.[9] In a related vein, Tom Allen studied proximity and found that the chances of people in an organization interacting with someone thirty meters outside their habitual paths at work is extremely low.[10] Instead, power in an organization has more to do with informal networks of people, shaped by their location as much as other forces such as formal responsibility.

These informal networks play important roles in decision making. Sometimes, the networks are visible and explicit. Other times, they are hidden and implicit, like whose office is near the bathroom. But you need to understand these networks to lead transformational change. Thus, one of the most important tools we use is nothing particularly special—we simply map the formal and informal decision structure to create awareness of how decisions are made. This tool may sound oversimplified or unworthy of attention, but too often, we assume that we know how decisions are made without understanding the full ecosystem of forces affecting our ability to transform. (The earlier discussion on folk theory gives one example of this lack of understanding.) To help you appreciate these ecosystems of forces, we suggest creating a *decision bottleneck map*.

How to Use Decision Bottleneck Maps

We call the map of how decisions are made in an organization the decision bottleneck map. To create one and use it, follow these steps outlined below.

1. *Map the explicit, formal decision-making structure.* This decision-making structure may be the same as the organization chart, or it may be different. But it is the organization's stated way of making decisions.

2. *Map the informal decision structure.* This map describes how decisions really happen inside an organization. To discover this practice, get out and talk with people inside your organization. Ask them, "How do things get done around here?" or "Who is important in making decisions about X?" You may also ask about a time when a decision wasn't carried

out. Encourage people to elaborate: "Tell me why that didn't go through as expected."

3. *Map out the related influences on the key decision.* Examine the support functions, like legal, purchasing, IT, or HR. Examine whether they will need to be involved in the decision and how.

As you build the decision bottleneck map, don't obsess about generating the perfect map. The goal isn't obsessive completeness. No one is grading you. Just focus on the important pieces and look for the moments of insight, however small, that the map is designed to uncover. For example, you may suddenly realize that "Bob" is the bottleneck on many decisions, even though he sits on the side in IT. When you realize this, you can ask, "What does Bob want?" and start to make progress breaking down this barrier. We have found that this simple tool, combined with the narrative, has incredible power to start and sustain transformation. Understanding the bottlenecks helps you know where to focus, and the narrative can help you win allies and enthusiasm.

But as you work with the decision bottleneck map and pay attention to the individuals in these bottlenecks, an analysis of each individual could become a burdensome chore. Rather, focus on the battles you need to win, and then unpack the functional archetypes of this smaller set of individuals, which will allow you to streamline the analysis to have maximum effect.

Tool: Functional Archetypes

One of the toughest bottlenecks we've ever dealt with was convincing a major electronics retailer to put robots in stores (the company and technology have been disguised to comply with a nondisclosure agreement). Although Lowe's had already successfully tested robots in stores, the head of the innovation lab at the electronics retailer applied the transformation process and discovered a different future: one in which robots could change the face of electronics retailing. For example, robots could assist by guiding customers around the store, giving them advice, helping them make decisions, and potentially even helping them put electronic systems together. (Envision a robot that could potentially assemble a smart home system of compatible products or even build a custom computer on the spot.) This kind of near-omniscient assistant could be both a disruptor of electronics retailing, with the ability to understand how the vast ecosystem of electronics products can work together in an increasingly integrated world, and a defense against low-cost online retailers because the robot would be able to provide deep insight and assistance in assembling systems unattainable from retailers like Amazon. Unfortunately, although executives had been excited about the project and given it a green light to proceed, the legal team had significant reservations that led to persistent delays.

Out of fairness to legal, you can imagine the concerns they might have. What if the robot injured someone in the store? Scared people? Led to resistance from people afraid they might lose their jobs? Gave improper advice to a customer, leading to poor reviews or an improperly functioning system? Assembled hardware that violated a manufacturer's warranty or patent? The objections were endless. Not surprisingly, both the legal and the risk teams became major bottlenecks to progress.

Meanwhile, in her eagerness, the head of the innovation lab, Natalie, had hired expensive roboticists and coders and begun building robot prototypes. Although the prototypes were under development, more meaningful progress had been held up by the inability to test in stores. At every turn, Natalie tried to push the legal team to approve the robots. But month after month, meeting after meeting, discussions with the legal team went nowhere.

Finally, in a moment of reflection, Natalie realized she hadn't been following two key steps of the transformation process itself.

First, she wasn't using the strategic narrative to share the company's vision of the future with the legal team. And second, she hadn't used the functional archetype tool to identify the legal department's strategic role in the company's transformation. As we describe in more detail later in this section, a functional archetype is a quick way to describe people's motivation for acting the way they do.

To remedy the situation, Natalie first took a closer look at the legal team. Although it was composed of many individuals in a rather tight-knit group, its functional role at the electronics company could be described as the *caretaker* archetype. Caretakers see their role as protecting the organization from threats and preserving the status quo. For caretakers, the robot in stores represented a massive threat. When Natalie had initially approached them, the legal team had considered her an attacker on the stronghold of their responsibility. Realizing that this adversarial relationship was not the way to persuade people, Natalie called a meeting with the legal team.

Reluctantly, the group assembled, with a few members arriving late. Around the room, the energy was low. People leaned back in chairs or typed away on their phones. Natalie cleared her throat. "I know we've been going in circles on this," she said, "but would you folks humor me a bit? Could we read the story that prompted all this in the first place? It's in a comic format, which I know isn't exactly a standard legal document, but it works well for telling the story. Could we read it first, then talk?" Natalie passed around the comic book, and people slowly started to thumb through it. As the team read, she could see people lean forward in their chairs or look more intently at the pages. The mood in the room started to change. As they finished reading, Natalie said, "The comic really just tells a vision of some of the things we could do at this company."

Then she did something critical—she reframed what she was doing in a language caretakers could appreciate: "But it isn't the only way. The really important thing is that the world is changing quickly around us, and how do we protect the company in the long run? By keeping up. I want to protect the company—nobody wants a big legal battle—but if we don't do anything, the company itself is in danger. As retail is changing so quickly, the big risk is doing nothing." Then she flipped the conversation around. Instead of treating them like service providers, she spoke to them as strategic partners: "I'm not saying that this is the only way to go or the only way to do it, but I need your help to figure out what's possible. Can you help me work out what we can do and what we can't do, so we don't become irrelevant in the future?"

The conversation that ensued totally surprised her. One team member spoke up. "Well, we could do this," one person said, describing one idea. Another jumped in and said, "This seems like another case that worked. We could draw on the precedent in that case." Soon other team members chimed in with ideas. The suggestions popping up drew on an impressive breadth of legal knowledge and proved thoughtful, usefully creative, and, quite frankly, brilliant.

The legal team left the meeting discussing how to make the robotics project work. And after months of zero progress, in just a few weeks, the team put together an opinion that paved the way for a groundbreaking perspective on robotics in retail operations. The legal framework proved so valuable that it represents one of their trade secrets.

Moreover, the legal team turned from seeming adversaries to powerful strategic partners. Afterward, the risk team and legal team members became some of the innovation lab's biggest advocates inside the company. (And when you get risk and legal on your side, that's really saying something!) Most important, the experience helped the legal team at the electronics company transform as well. Developing the ability to see what is possible, rather than what is impossible, has become part of the legal team culture at the company. In one particularly memorable moment, as Natalie walked past a new recruit being introduced to the legal team, she overheard something that brought joy to her heart. "Rachel," the legal team member said, "working here is going to feel different than anything you have done before. And that's a good thing!" It is a good thing. The electronics company was making a profound transformation both in terms of what they offered to customers and how it operated.

How to Use Functional Archetypes

One tool we recommend for breaking bottlenecks is to assess the functional archetypes of the people you are trying to work with. Before we dive into functional archetypes, we have to ask, What drives behavior? The answer is that a thousand things influence human behavior. Sometimes, people simplify these thousand things into nature or nurture, but even this dichotomy starts to break down under the scrutiny of imaging genetics, a new field that lies at the intersection of genetics and neuroscience. The field of imaging genetics explores how your genetic traits combine with your experiences to shape your decisions. For example, about 20 percent of the population has the gene for a particular serotonin transporter that leads to an excess of serotonin, an important neurotransmitter, at the synapse (the place where two neurons meet). Having this gene will lead you to be more anxious and more loss averse. Combine that with a personal history in which unsettling things happened with no warning, and you are likely to become risk-averse.[11] This is not to say that you have no choice in becoming risk-averse, but you do have a higher likelihood of becoming risk-averse than does someone without that gene but with the same life experience.

Why share this example? Simply to acknowledge that why and how we make decisions are probably best mapped out as probabilities shaped by complex interactions of genes, history, learning, context, and many other factors. But mapping these complex forces makes for an unwieldy way of understanding the world. Fortunately, in a world before neuroscience, imaging genetics, or personality scales, observers of human nature roughly categorized the roles people play in terms of archetypes. Often forming the backbone of many powerful stories, archetypes underlie some of the most influential early studies in psychology.[12] Although these archetypes are grossly oversimplified, in many ways, modern psychology and neuroscience still support the mechanisms for how these archetypes work (see "Master Class: Neuroscience, Archetypes, and the Real World").

We use archetypes as shorthand for describing the reasons that some people act the way they do in their functional roles and how to persuade them when change is required. For example, in the story about the legal team at the electronics company, we highlighted several critical elements relevant to breaking bottlenecks. For example, as we examine more closely later in the chapter, we turned insiders into uncommon partners rather than seeing them as a means to an end. More importantly, the story describes how recognizing a core archetype in organizations helped us overcome the bottleneck. In the electronics company case, the people in the legal team weren't being difficult. They were just doing their jobs. They saw themselves as caretakers, tasked to protect the company from risks.

Whenever you approach a caretaker with a big, risky initiative, the person will, without realizing it, find ways to deflect or reject it. To work with a caretaker, you need to reframe the initiative so that it fulfills the caretaker's role. Working with the legal team on the robotics proposal, Natalie reframed the situation in the language of a caretaker. She argued that as the retail world faces increasing threats of disruption, the real risk was sitting idle and doing nothing. Finally, she used the strategic narrative to motivate the team members on what was possible and asked them to help us take care of the organization. The bottleneck broke immediately.

Below we describe how to use individual archetypes to break down barriers in your organization.

1. *Identify the functional archetypes of the individuals in your bottleneck map.* Classify the individuals who sit in key decision points in the bottleneck map in terms of their primary functional archetype (the role they play in that position). For a list of key archetypes, see table 3-3. Don't waste time endlessly mapping out every archetype onto every individual in the organization or debating exactly which archetype someone is. Instead, focus on the bottlenecks necessary to do your work and then focus on these.

2. *Classify your own archetype.* Be careful about how you are perceived. Often, innovators or transformation leaders are seen as thieves (they steal time, money, focus, or turf from others in the organization) or tricksters (they aren't really doing anything productive for the organization). If you are seen this way, the image can damage your ability to get things done and you may need to reshape your archetype. When Kyle discovered the utility of functional archetypes, he purposefully reshaped his image as the magician (the magician always delivers some tangible, useful magic). He already looked the part and, most importantly, he always came to every meeting with some magic: a new technology, device, or insight he could pull out of his backpack. The gifts he brought underscored his role as a magician.

3. *Discover what the other archetypes value.* Use the language of the archetype you are working with, and work toward their values. For example, when Natalie talked about putting the first drone into a warehouse, the CEO valued boldly carving new territory. This awareness of his functional archetype helped her win his support. Later, when it came time to convince other leaders, her knowledge of their different archetypes helped her break through the decision bottlenecks by delivering the things they valued to them.

TABLE 3-3

Key functional archetypes

Archetype	Motto	Description	Key values	Dislikes
Hero	"Where there's a will, there's a way"	Strives to improve the organization through mastery and strength	Having impact, saving the day, worthwhile missions, skill mastery, competence	Vulnerability, weakness, quitting
Outlaw	"Rules are meant to be broken"	Challenges the organization to do more	Disruption, change, transformation, breaking norms	Trivialized, inconsequential, conformist attitudes
Magician	"It can happen"	Figures out how something works and applies it in the organization to get things done	Technology, advancement, understanding, visionary attitude, creating the future	Unexpected negative consequences
Explorer	"Don't fence me in"	Leads organization to a better world	New activities, new initiatives, new markets, adventure	Trapped settings, routines, conformity
Innocent	"Free to be you and me"	Tries to make the organization an ideal place	Simplicity, harmony, traditional values, utopian ideals, carefulness	Doing something wrong or against the norm
Sage	"The truth will set you free"	Creates superior knowledge in the organization	Intelligence, insight, knowledge, frameworks, expertise, wisdom, mentorship	Being deceived, intellectual vacuity
Caregiver	"Protect against all danger"	Protects the organization from risk and danger	Avoiding risk, protecting, preserving, helping, developing	Risks, novelty, selfishness
Creator	"If it can be imagined, it can be created"	Helps organization create something of enduring value	Design, beauty, meaning, artistic skill, loyalty to creative values	Sloppy design, poor execution, limited vision

Ruler	"Power is everything"	Creates a prosperous organization through control	Leadership, direction, control, order, stability, heritage	Chaos, subversion, disobedience
Regulator	"All people are created equal"	Fosters a cooperative organization	Cooperation, consensus, straightforwardness, thrift, conservatism	Elitism, rejection, exclusion
Lover	"I care for you"	Develops an organization that cares deeply	Commitment, compassion, passion, appreciation, harmony, team building	Disinterest, isolation, discord
Jester	"I want to have fun"	Creates an enjoyable atmosphere in the company	Fun, play, humor, lightheartedness, enjoyment, cleverness	Boredom, routine

Source: Adapted from Margaret Mark and Carol S. Pearson, *The Hero and the Outlaw: Building Extraordinary Brands Through the Power of Archetypes* (New York: McGraw Hill Professional, 2001).

Note: Mottos are direct quotations from Mark and Pearson, *The Hero and the Outlaw*; archetypes and other elements of text are inspired by Mark and Pearson, *The Hero and the Outlaw*, and as originally suggested by Carl Gustav Jung, *The Archetypes and the Collective Unconscious* (London: Routledge, 2014).

Master Class: Neuroscience, Archetypes, and the Real World

Why do some children who are traumatized during childhood go on to become violent offenders whereas others live out peaceful lives? Is it just a matter of choice? As one of us (Thomas) argues in "How Genes Make Up Your Mind," people need to go beyond the binary nature-nurture debate of the human mind.[13] Decisions are the result of a mashup between our genes, life history, and learning. With the advent of imaging genetics we are getting much closer to understanding the underlying causes of our behavior.

Today, the age-old answers of who we are and why we have a certain personality trait are becoming more tangible than ever. For example, if one child exposed to a traumatic event has a certain variant of the so-called MAO-A (monoamine oxidase A) gene expressed, then the probability of his or her turning violent is quite high, whereas the child experiencing the same thing with a different version of the MAO-A gene is unlikely to become violent. Likewise, a person who has the "bad" version of the MAO-A gene but is not exposed to trauma is not more likely to develop aggression.

These forces affect major life courses just as much as they affect small decisions. For example, in another study, Thomas and his colleagues used fMRI brain scanning to understand how we are affected by cues when we are making social judgments and decisions.[14] First, they showed that, by framing an exercise a certain way, the researchers could change how people played the famous prisoner's dilemma game (where people have to decide whether to rat out a colleague in another prison cell in exchange for better treatment). On average, 61 percent of people would collaborate with their co-conspirator if they were told it was a cooperative game, compared with a 29 percent cooperation rate if they were told it was a competitive game.

But these figures are just the averages! The real force explaining who cooperates and who does not is actually the relative engagement of the social area of the brain, sometimes referred to as the *mentalizing network* because it is engaged whenever we are thinking about others' states of mind. People who scored higher on an empathy test showed faster response times to social cues, were better at predicting what their coconspirators were going to do, and showed increased activity in the brain's memory and emotional regions. Most important, people with greater empathy scores made up the gap between the competitive and cooperative states—more empathetic people were the ones switching to play collaboratively during a cooperative game. This suggested that individual differences in the level of empathy could explain why some people were faster and more accurate at navigating social decision environments: their brains were more acutely tuned to think and act fast. Participants with greater empathy explained the increase.[15]

Although we have used archetypes as shorthand to describe people's roles in organizations, one could better represent their behavior with scales that show the probability of certain choices. Moreover, although these scales are shaped by people's genes, they are also deeply affected by life history and learning. For example, Thomas's research team developed a creative-potential test battery, which is based on a set of creativity scales, and then showed that simply explaining the neuroscience elements of creativity to people increased their creativity by 30 percent on average (a range of 15 to 200 percent).[16] In the future, it will be possible to go beyond creativity and instead develop a set of scales that predict probabilistically how people will respond to forces such as persuasion, framing, and decision making based on their genes, life experience, and related factors. The corollary to these predictors would be a set of scales to understand your own behavior as well as a set of tools to help amplify or counteract these natural tendencies. In other words, we could increase the power you have over the choices you make and your ability to influence others.

Caveats and Alternatives: A Major Rule—Don't Tell Everyone

Although we talk about becoming aware of the archetypes of the decision makers who become bottlenecks, we do follow one important rule: don't tell everyone what you are doing. In fact, we encourage you to tell as few people as possible about what you are doing. Why? First, the more people you tell, the greater the number of people who want to get involved, inject their own opinions, and ultimately slow the process down. You will have to involve people and key functions at different points, and later in the book, we'll share some ideas on how to involve them. But don't involve everyone from the start. Second, the more people you tell, the greater the likelihood that you start setting high expectations for what you will accomplish (see "Master Class: The Dangers of Setting and Revising Expectations with Narratives" in chapter 2). Setting high expectations among a large group of onlookers can be very dangerous since in anything truly transformational, there will be a great deal of uncertainty and ultimately there will be change. You want to preserve your flexibility to adjust as needed.

Tool: Bottleneck Breakers

Ultimately, breaking bottlenecks comes down to identifying the functional archetypes of the key decision makers and then delivering to these people whatever they need to join you in creating transformational change. This approach may sound a bit jaded, but it isn't—we just recognize that organizations are made up of people, most of whom are trying their best to play the role they think they should play. So you need both to help them play the role well and to see their role in a new way. There should be nothing inauthentic or deceptive in your attempt to clear roadblocks to a transformation. You should be earnestly trying to help everyone achieve the best collective outcome. To this end, we'll share a couple of favorite bottleneck breakers. Although the list isn't exhaustive (some we even share in other chapters), it covers several tools you can use both inside and outside the organization to get past these barriers.

Third-Party Digital Arbiter

Recently a major retailer ran into a perplexing mystery (identities have been disguised). Consumers suddenly seemed to stop buying a major product: oranges. The result was massive overstocks. No one could figure out the sudden change. Had customers changed their preferences? Was it a pricing issue? An advertising issue? The puzzle persisted until a junior manager (nicknamed Kate) at the organization did some simple data analysis comparing sales trends over multiple years with various Google search terms. Kate discovered an obvious phenomenon that everyone had overlooked. When a series of successive flu seasons had led to an increase in orange sales, everyone had assumed the surge in sales was a long-term trend. In fact, it was only the result of a compounding series of flu seasons! Because the data was so self-evident, no one argued with the findings. Instead, leaders just mobilized to take the next step.

The experience with the power of data to uncover behavior patterns and eliminate unproductive politics sparked Kate's curiosity. The retailer where Kate worked had an area of the store dedicated to new items not sold as part of the regular inventory. She began to wonder if there might be hidden patterns in this area of the store as well. Taking the data on sales, she began to look for patterns, for example, items that few people tried, but that they loyally repurchased (low trial, high repeat purchase). She quickly discovered problems in the way items were displayed, packaged, or sold. Using the data to uncover and then talk about a problem took much of the venom out of potentially contentious debates. Instead, the organization could spend its energy on solving the problem. What Kate discovered was the power of data linked to behavior to generate insight and to arbitrate challenging political debates.

We recently had our own experience using data as a third-party digital arbiter to break bottlenecks in another setting. A major retailer had been trying to optimize its light bulb sales for years. Because powerful suppliers like Philips and GE fought (and sometimes paid) for shelf space, the lighting aisle was arranged by brand. But if you have ever walked into a big store looking for a light bulb, you know by experience how unhelpful this arrangement can be. A $1 light bulb may be sitting next to a $25 light bulb, both of which are different from the actual bulb you are looking for. Although it might make sense to arrange light bulbs differently, doing so was a major political issue. But as customers grew more confused with every increase in choice, we proposed a simple experiment. We tested two alternative arrangements for light bulbs: one with the bulbs arranged by price and the other arranged by type. After gathering the data on sales, we then used a simple machine-learning algorithm (the free software tool TensorFlow) to parse the resulting data and create an optimal model.

Which of the three layouts—brand, price, or type—do you think was the optimal for generating sales? None of them! The algorithm suggested that the optimal layout would draw on a combination of the price and type layouts (and nothing from the brand layout). Using the data and the machine learning led to a productive discussion, with the data as a third-party digital arbiter of the argument. We could discuss whether the model was right, not whether individuals were right. We then retested the new model in stores to continued success.

The experience illustrates the power of data as a bottleneck breaker. Big organizations love data, particularly quantitative data. They love data over time even more, especially data trends (hopefully, improving data trends). But combining data with models that describe how to use the data may be even better. Instead of arguing about who was right, the model becomes a third-party digital intermediary to take the venom and politics out of an issue and instead to encourage a discussion about whether the model is right. If you then combine this data with applied neuroscience (discussed in chapter 4), you can truly understand what the data is saying.

Turn Abundance into Currency

How did Lowe's, the DIY retailer, get some of the world's leading tech companies, such as Google, Microsoft, and Lenovo, to work with it? And how did Lowe's persuade these companies to trade significant development resources in exchange for what they really wanted? The key to getting this kind of access and value was to turn Lowe's overlooked abundance into currency. Let us explain.

As humans, we tend to overvalue whatever we have little of and undervalue what we have in abundance. Among the many resources Lowe's had undervalued were the thousands of stores that host millions of customers each week, each person walking in with an unspoken social contract that he or she wants to learn and is willing to engage. The eagerness of abundant customers proved an ideal environment to test ideas with them. The turning point came when Lowe's learned to take this initial abundance and convert it and other sources of abundance the retailer had created (data, digital-imaging capability, etc.) into currency to build true partnerships that money can't buy.

Every company has some abundance that could somehow be eventually turned into currency. Look for your sources of abundance—the things you have but possibly undervalue. For example, physical locations can be chances to learn from customers or can become distribution platforms, sales outlets, space for partners, rentable square footage, and more. International locations can provide you greater flexibility in testing new technologies or a space off the radar to explore ideas. Language capabilities can give you local access that partners crave or can never imitate. Other companies have an abundance of customer understanding, and yet others have an abundance of data—a richness that they just don't recognize. Even companies that think they have no abundance often can find it or create it. For example, when Kyle combined the Lowe's testing environment with the data generated using applied neuroscience tools, the combination of assets and capabilities multiplied the value of the retailer's abundance.

Turning Insiders into Uncommon Partners: The Justice League

One good way to handle internal resistance is to find other initiatives in your organization to tag-team with. At the electronics company mentioned earlier, we discovered a way to do just that—ultimately converting a potential source of resistance, IT, into an uncommon partner. Although the head of the innovation lab, Natalie, had received executive approval to scale up the robotics concepts after some very promising proof-of-concept work, she was having trouble connecting with IT to get started on the project.

In one meeting, Natalie explained the robotics and some of the IT needs to scale it up, including the ability to link the robotics systems into the ever-evolving database of products sold and their characteristics.

The IT director just shook his head in silence. Finally, he said, "I can't do it. It's not in the road map."

Natalie paused. "Yes, but at the CEO staff meeting, they approved scaling this up."

Continuing to shake his head, the director replied, "It's not in the roadmap. It would take a totally different system and budget that I don't have."

By the end of the tense meeting, Natalie and the director were no closer to a resolution, and the director suggested she check with the e-commerce department for available resources. Natalie began to wonder what could be done.

At the same time, the business development organization within the company was continually looking for the right approach to successfully build new initiatives that could scale into the core of the business. The head of the group asked Natalie for a recommendation on how the innovation lab team might approach this problem. Because we had been working with Natalie, we suggested that she form a cross-functional team similar to DC Comics's Justice League team. In the Justice League series, rotating casts of superheroes come together to solve a single problem. Afterward, they disband and reassemble in different combinations (for one challenge, it may be Wonder Woman and for another it may be Superman). The Justice League would be a team of "superheroes" from each function—people who, working together, could tackle this problem and make more progress, faster?

In the first embodiment of the Justice League, Natalie visited each of the major functions. She shared the robotics story, showed the latest prototypes, and then asked for their help: "This company has the chance to redefine the future of electronics retailing. But we need your help figuring out how to do it. We want to create a team of our best to define a sixty-day sprint to figure out if and how to turn our vision for robotics into reality. Since this is critical to everyone in the company, could you nominate the high potentials who should be part of the team? We are calling the team the Justice League, and just like in the movies, they are the heroes who can define the future. This is an initiative that has support from the top executive team and it is a major honor to participate."

As recommendations started to trickle in from different parts of the organization, Natalie worked hard to make the Justice League a high-profile, prestigious assignment. She gave out T-shirts, figurines, and "Justice League" bags. In short order, Natalie assembled a team of high potentials from each of the major functions. She then took the newly formed Justice League team for an off-site to define the sprint about what to do next. At the end of the off-site, the high potentials from each function presented their recommendations. Because the Justice League was composed of a cross-functional team of high potentials, suddenly, the initiative was not just an innovation lab project. It was everyone's project. As the Justice League team stood and presented, the executives in each division took note. These were their best and brightest, and their ideas were quite good and grounded in the realities of each function.

Why did the Justice League program work? It worked, in part, because it created uncommon partners out of internal functions. Sometimes it's easier to collaborate with the National Aeronautics and Space Administration (NASA) than it is to work with someone you don't know in another function. The Justice League turned the functions we normally treat like supporting actors into partners and made it easy to collaborate. It also worked because the participants, like the comic-book Justice League, used their special skills in harmony to solve a critical puzzle. The program also created prestige and motivation for the participants. Being on the team was framed as a significant honor and one of the few indicators that someone was a high potential. Moreover, the participants received visible symbols of their participation, so the best people felt highly motivated to be a part of it. Finally, the program worked because, at the end of the week, the high-potential people inside a function recommended to their own function what should be done. The high potentials in accounting were presenting to the accounting executives just as the high potentials in IT were presenting to their own function's executives. By creating partners out of critical functions, you can break down overwhelming barriers to transformation.

Speak the Value Language

The power of speaking the same language of the group we are trying to influence is worth mentioning again. Too often, we forget to speak in the value language of the resisting group. When O'Neill spoke to Alcoa about taking care of workers, he was speaking in the organization's value language. When Natalie spoke to the legal team about protecting their company, she was speaking in its value language.

So how can you learn to speak an organization's or individual's value language? Try this. First, identify someone who is your adversary or who is in your way. Next, ask yourself, what do people like this want? Ask yourself not what you want them to do, but what their incentives are. What is driving these people? Finally, ask yourself, How do I communicate what I am trying to do in terms of their incentives? In the electronics company legal team case, the team saw its job as protecting and advancing the company's interests, so we reframed our transformation efforts by helping the team members see that it is a risk not to take risks.

Reframe the Purpose

Framing means recasting an idea or activity with the words you use to describe it, and the choice of framing can completely change how people make decisions. The importance of framing is not new news. We've been talking about this already. But rarely do we appreciate how much framing can change our decisions. For example, behavioral economist Daniel Ariely describes how when people are given the choice of purchasing a trip to Rome or to Paris, about half of the people will choose Rome and half will choose Paris. But when the choice is framed as an easy comparison between purchasing a trip to Rome, a trip to Rome with breakfast included, and a trip to Paris, most people will choose Rome because it is easier to compare the value of Rome with breakfast and without breakfast.[17] Not only can framing change the way we make decisions, but framing can also even override deeply held values, such as political beliefs. For example, in a recent experiment by Oberlin professor Paul Thibodeau and his collaborator Lera Boroditsky, participants were told about a crime wave affecting the city and were asked how to deal with it. For half the participants, the crime wave was described as a "beast preying" on the city, and for the other half, it was described as a "virus infecting" the city. Although every other piece of information in the dossier was identical for the two groups, that simple metaphor (beast versus virus) overrode people's native political views about how to deal with social problems like crime. Those in the "beast" category overwhelmingly prescribed more punishment for crimes, and those in the virus category prescribed more preventative measures.[18] In short, framing has immense power. As you seek to create a transformation, we strongly recommend that you frame your purpose to match the goals of the archetype you are working with.

Making the Transformation Tangible

We are all unduly persuaded by tangible artifacts or small wins. In chapter 4, we will talk about the artifact trail, whose goal is explicitly to make the transformation tangible. But making ideas tangible is so important, it needs to be called out separately from the artifact trail. It is no accident that Elon Musk, who struggled to get NASA's attention, later won billions of dollars in NASA contracts after he drove the first Space X rocket across the country and parked it in front of FAA headquarters during its centenary celebration of the Wright Brothers. The attendees seeing the rocket with their own eyes made them believers!

We recommend using as many tangible artifacts and small wins as possible—they will help remove barriers. What do we mean by tangible artifacts? Start small, and eventually think big. The comic book is a tangible artifact. So are the prototypes. So are partners signed up to help you. So is progress on the future KPIs you will create in the next chapter. When the three of us are trying to break a decision bottleneck, we are always leaving bits of technology sitting out on our own desks and dropping it off to others to show them what is possible and to make it real. We also try to accumulate small wins—small proof points, bits of positive feedback, connections to prestigious partners, awards, or any other achievement to help the doubters believe what is possible.

Summary

We opened this chapter by describing the power of routine to create bottlenecks in the organization. We then described the tools we use for overcoming these barriers. The tools involved first identifying the *organizational nomenclature*—what the organization values (although few people probably ever talk about this out loud). With this self-awareness, you then create a *decision bottleneck map* that describes the formal, informal, and supporting decision-making structure in the organization. Next, you identify the *functional archetypes* of the individuals who can block the transformation effort so that you can understand how to influence them. Finally, you consider how to apply a *bottleneck breaker*, of which several were described.

In describing the process we followed, we meant only to provide tools designed to counteract the biasing force of habit. Our list of tools is not exhaustive or fail-proof. Use your own judgment about how and when to best use these tools. For example, in chapter 4, we describe how to use applied neuroscience to generate the kind of data that executives, customers, or partners won't or can't tell you. This data can also be fundamental to addressing barriers to transformation. So although we describe our overall transformation process using three discrete steps—strategic narrative, breaking bottlenecks, and using fKPIs for creating the future—don't be afraid to use the tools in the order that helps you create transformational change.

FOUR

Navigating the Unknown

*Using Applied Neuroscience and
Future Key Performance Indicators (fKPIs)*

As the world's population continues to grow, so will the pressure on energy, food, and other natural resources, especially if human society collectively succeeds at lifting people out of poverty into reasonable living standards. Where will the energy come from when burning more carbon amplifies climate unpredictability? Where will the protein come from when there simply aren't enough animals to feed the population? Where will the textiles, metals, woods, and plastics come from to build housing and products for this population?

With these questions in mind, IKEA recently created a strategic narrative that led the company to ask some radical, disruptive, and even outlandish questions about its business: What if instead of just selling home furnishings, they also sold solutions that helped resolve these tensions? For example, instead of just selling ovens, should IKEA also sell customers renewable power? If IKEA sold them electricity, should they allow customers to invest in energy, subscribe to energy, or manage their energy? Or should IKEA go further and truly enable customers to take control of their energy needs? IKEA could do so by creating virtual power grids that are based on blockchain and that allow customer communities to trade power with each other. IKEA could even give access to renewables to customers living in apartments (i.e., people who don't own a roof and who thus cannot install solar units). Could electricity be free if the business model were structured in a different way? Can IKEA provide access to clean water from more-responsible sources? Should IKEA turn their urban customers into farmers, allowing them to grow food close to the source and supply local restaurants or even IKEA's own restaurants? Each of these questions was both radical and inspiring in relation to IKEA's historical identity and its familiar business model.

If you were working as IKEA's consultant, what would you advise it to do? Perhaps you might think the company is getting a bit off-kilter, and if you were raised in the core-capabilities view of business, you might remind the company to stay closer to its familiar business model. But how would you know if you were right? The world is dramatically changing. A billion more people will join the human race in the next ten years, and the population will almost double by the end of the century. What if one of these new initiatives proved incredibly valuable and completely disrupted the retail or utility industry and at the same time met your vision as a company? If you were raised in the disruption view of the world, you would see these changes as a necessity, not a choice, and remind people that they must disrupt or be disrupted. But which among all these choices is the right way to go? Although you might recommend something in light of a past example or framework you have in mind, the truth is, you can't know. Past data won't clearly predict the future. How could you discover which way to go while defending yourself from the internal skeptics pushing back because of fear?

Experimental design, or the use of reliable experiments to generate reliable metrics, can guide us under uncertainty. In the IKEA case, we employed applied neuroscience—a new field that provides precise, data-driven measures of user reactions and thereby allows you to understand unspoken, subconscious reactions. Using high-resolution EEG headsets and eye trackers, all of which feel a bit like wearing a baseball cap, we tested IKEA customers in Poland and the Netherlands to understand their reactions to the new business models. We then correlated their reactions with a huge behavioral database to pinpoint which business models they were likely to accept, to never accept, or to adopt in a few years, given some time to adjust. These experimental design tools gave Håkan Nordkvist, head of sustainability innovation at IKEA Group, and a true champion for changing the world, a shortcut to understanding the emotions and reactions that will drive one business model over another. Nordkvist has used these tools and other experimental design methods in combination with the company's strategic narrative to create successful new business models at IKEA. The models include a home solar offering that enables customers to generate their own renewable energy, a shift to renewable plastics, and innovations that provide customers at the IKEA restaurant chain choices of healthier and more-sustainable food.

Many organizations talk about experiments, and many leaders may feel they are experimenting. But these leaders are finding that to take advantage of the true power of experimental design, they need to provide data-driven key performance indicators that help them navigate the future, or what we will call future KPIs (fKPI). These indicators have the power both to guide their organizations through the unknown and to convince adamant skeptics. Creating these metrics is critical to transformation since one of the most powerful forces holding back all change is fear. This chapter shows how to do just that.

The Need: Tools to Overcome the Fear of the Unknown

For individuals and organizations, the challenge of trying to transform—whether it be embracing new technology, strategies, business models, or other changes—is the fear of the unknown. As humans, we are wired with an intense, evolutionary-based aversion to both risk and uncertainty. A recent study by California Institute of Technology scientists showed that risk and uncertainty are actually two separate neural reactions, each having a major impact on our choices.[1] Moreover, in a structure known as the amygdala, deep within the center of the brain, choices with ambiguous outcomes trigger a stronger fear response than do risky choices. Engagement of the amygdala is known to lead to a cascade of bodily and behavioral responses, such as palm sweating, increased pulse and respiration, and dilation of the pupils, as well as avoidance behaviors such as looking away, leaning backward, and running away. These distinct reactions help explain why uncertainty and risk are so hard to deal with—we have negative reactions to both, but uncertainty, or the inability to predict the outcome, creates deep, visceral fear of its own.[2] Likewise, a separate study, this time rooted in psychology, compared participants choosing between outcomes with different levels of uncertainty. The results underscored that the risk itself isn't so much the problem, but the uncertainty is: we are afraid primarily because we don't know the outcome, and less so because of the risk.[3]

The dilemma is that every transformation means going into uncertain territory where there are few signposts to create confidence that you are heading in the right direction. As a result, onlookers and skeptics may hesitate to join you or even resist you. Moreover, it can be a massive emotional challenge to maintain your confidence when you have few points of feedback yourself. The strategic narrative can provide the initial confidence to start the transformation and the direction to go, but to succeed, you need to generate reliable, defensible, data-driven KPIs that give you confidence that both you and your organization are heading in the right direction.

The Process: Using Experimental Design and Applied Neuroscience to Create fKPIs to Navigate the Unknown

As described earlier, Lowe's began developing AR and VR experiences back in 2012, before Oculus Rift had been purchased by Facebook, long before Pokémon Go, and during the period when people remembered AR and VR as overhyped vaporware from the 1990s. How Lowe's navigated its way through the uncertain terrain of the early days, when few companies were investing—most certainly not home improvement companies—and then how it wove through the confusing hubbub of hype that eventually exploded around the technology illustrates the process for experimental design in the future.

After creating a narrative-based vision for how AR and VR could change the future of retail, telling the story in comics, and navigating the hurdles inside Lowe's to win support, we still had to resolve the two critical uncertainties: Could we make the technology in the story, and would customers use it? We began by defining the *artifact trail*, the series of small steps from concept to grand vision. We described the fast, small, easy-win activities, then the prototypes of increasing fidelity, and, ultimately, the final outcome. The artifact trail created team confidence in how to move forward and critical evidence to skeptics that the Innovation Labs at Lowe's was making real progress.

After laying out the artifact trail, we defined the experimental design, a well-established set of scientific protocols that we try to make accessible in what today we call the *experimental design canvas*. The experimental design canvas helps you define the most important measures to guide your choices and convince your skeptics, as well as how to generate the data for those measures. Because

we were exploring a very new space—AR and VR—and were trying to move quickly, we opted for applied neuroscience in our experimental design. This scientific tool can help anyone go beyond
what people say they like; you can see what they actually want.[4]
Indeed, the systems of liking and wanting are actually distinct in
the brain, with want both preceding the feeling of liking and providing more-accurate guidance to human behavior, since liking is
often hard to express or even is an inaccurate feeling when one is
facing new things.

Once we had defined an experimental design, we quickly started
putting together crude prototypes, for example, an iPad that you
could point at a room and then superimpose virtual objects wher-
ever you placed a QR code in the room (to see this prototype, watch
Kyle's Tedx talk). This and other prototypes were crude and clumsy
compared with today's AR, but they helped convince skeptics that
it could be done, and they helped start the learning process. Most
importantly, Kyle and his team had defined the metrics and an
experimental design that could reveal what was working, or not.
This meant we could verify that the customer's positive emotional
engagement matched up with their stated improvement in confidence to take on a home improvement project.

Using these clues about where to go next, we then developed numerous prototypes as we advanced along the artifact trail to the
most recent version. These prototypes included multiple versions of
the Holoroom, beginning with the iPad-based AR device and evolving from what we had learned to include VR and mixed-reality
design and visualization experiences (figure 4-1).[5] Next, we explored
a series of phone-based applications, beginning by giving away
branded Google Cardboard devices as Holoroom extensions and
then becoming a development partner for Google's Tango platform
for AR. Next, we debuted the Lowe's Vision application and began
selling the Lenovo Phab2Pro Tango-equipped smartphone at
Lowe's. By the time Apple and Android had released their new AR
platforms (ARKit and ARCore, respectively) to millions of users

FIGURE 4-1

Holoroom prototype

Source: Lowe's, "Science Fiction Inspires Lowe's Holoroom and Home Improvement Innovation," PR Newswire, June 11, 2014, https://www.prnewswire.com/news-releases/science-fiction-inspires-lowes -holoroom-and-home-improvement-innovation-262717851.html.

around the world in 2017, Lowe's had more experience with AR and VR than did any other retailer on the planet. The company was ready with a suite of applications that helped customers with various projects, from simple measurements to complex designs.

Sometimes, the experimental design suggested what was not working—information that led us to remove features or to take initially counterintuitive directions. (For example, in related studies we have learned that although it would seem logical to increase the fidelity of the digital objects as much as possible, it actually helped to find the optimal balance between fidelity and how long it takes to put a 3-D object into the scene.[6] The idea was to avoid slow-loading issues that would cause consumers to lose patience.)

The experimental design also occasionally led us to change direction. For example, we moved from a focus on VR to AR as a design and visualization tool, while continuing to push VR in new directions for learning and training. Whereas the Holoroom VR application often left consumers wishing they could see changes in

FIGURE 4-2

Augmented-reality example

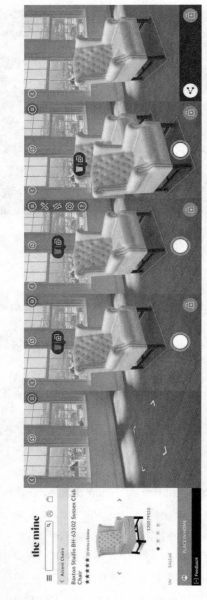

Source: Lowe's Companies, Inc., "Lowe's Gives Visualization a Makeover with Two New Augmented Reality Apps," PR Newswire, September 25, 2017, https://www.prnewswire.com/news-releases/lowes-gives-visualization-a-makeover-with-two-new-augmented-reality-apps-300524640.html.

their own space, smartphone-based AR proved to be an intuitive tool for customers to use at home. Users could measure the dimensions of a space by simply pointing the phone at the room and then could superimpose virtual objects onto their physical space to get a sense of what a remodel might look like (figure 4-2). At the same time, the immersive nature of VR made it the perfect environment to train customers and employees on DIY skills, leading Lowe's to develop the Holoroom How To experience.

By the time the Tango platform was launched, we had neuro-prototyped it, along with many other technologies on the market: Oculus Rift, Microsoft Hololens, Google Cardboard, HTC Vive, and many others. We knew something that only the experimental design could reveal: responses to the latest smartphone-based AR design tools were associated with a high motivation score both when the customers were anticipating using the tool and when they were actually using it. The customers' cognitive load was well within the sweet spot for engagement and surpassed any other solution we had tried at the time. These results indicated a greater likelihood that customers would adopt the AR design tool. This insight was the root of a truly uncommon partnership between Lowe's and Google.

When Kyle met with Google after the launch of the Holoroom in Canada in 2014, Lowe's seemed like an unlikely partner for the technology giant. He explained Lowe's future-facing projects to the Google team: "At Lowe's, we are building robots, mixed reality, 3-D printing services, and other futuristic technologies. But we don't build them in the dark. We use science fiction to inspire where to go and then incorporate experimental design, including applied neuroscience, to test if we are going in the right direction, and we make data-driven pivots to build the future." As Kyle began to show the progress Lowe's had made and some of the neuroscience data the group had gathered, the Googlers started to sit up in their chairs. Some started texting their colleagues to come into the meeting. The room started to fill up. Kyle continued to explain how they had tested many solutions, and the neuroscience data revealed how consumers currently found different VR devices overwhelming. Kyle said that customers' familiarity with smartphones, and the ability to quickly shift their gaze when they needed a break, made smartphone-based AR the most likely of the technologies to be picked up by users in the near term.

At the end of the meeting, the Google AR team was buzzing. After Kyle left the room, the discussion continued: "How do we start using these tools ourselves? We should be working with Lowe's." Surprisingly, Lowe's was now delivering actionable strategic insights to Google.

In the next section, we describe the tools you can use to create confidence as you navigate the unknown. We'll examine the benefits of creating an artifact trail as a pathway to the future (and creating the small wins that build confidence in the direction you are heading). We'll look at then using the experimental design canvas to define the right KPIs to guide you and create confidence among your onlookers. Although we don't describe every kind of experimental mechanism, we briefly consider a few and then focus on applied neuroscience, with which we have extensive experience as the baseline for neuroprototyping. Finally, we discuss how to use these KPIs to understand real behavior using a behavioral database that you can access or build yourself. Ultimately, the purpose of this chapter is to provide the tools you need to overcome the fear-based resistance that almost always accompanies transformation.

Tool: Artifact Trail

One of the greatest challenges in creating new futures is the paralyzing fear that accompanies unknown territory. The impact of this fear, and its remedy, may be best illustrated by a now-famous story reportedly recounted by Nobel Prize–winning biochemist Albert Szent-Györgyi. During World War I, a company of Hungarian soldiers was camped high in the Alps. Concerned about enemy soldiers nearby, the young lieutenant in charge sent out a small scouting party. Unfortunately, soon after the scouting party left, the snow began to fall hard and fast. As the snow deepened and night fell, the scouting party did not return. Nor did they return the next day. Or the next. With every passing day, the young lieutenant's agony over his decision increased. He began to torture himself with questions: Weren't they young men, like himself, with hopes and dreams? Why had he sent them needlessly to their deaths? Why were they even fighting this war high in the Alps?

On the third day, as the lieutenant continued to brood, suddenly he heard shouts. It was the scouting party returning to camp! Everyone rushed out to greet the men, cheering with excitement and relief. But perhaps no one was more relieved than the young lieutenant. He pressed in to speak to the group's leader, asking, "What happened? Where were you? How did you make it back?" Breathing hard from the ascent, the leader of the scouting party told how they had become hopelessly lost in the snow. After wandering endlessly, freezing and starving, they had resigned themselves to die. But then, as one scouting party member searched for paper to write a final letter home, he found a map of the mountains in his pocket! With renewed hope, the scouting party followed the map and made it back safely. Amazed, the lieutenant eagerly asked to see the map they had used. Taking the map in his trembling hands, he held it for a moment, turned it, turned it again, and looked up. "This is a map of the Pyrenees, not the Alps!"[7]

Although the story has been told many times and interpreted in different ways, it is often retold because it demonstrates how we can be paralyzed by uncertainty and its accompanying fear. The story also shows the power of moving forward even though the pathway may not be exactly right. The map gives people the confidence to start moving.

To counter the debilitating fear that almost always accompanies transformation, we try to create a map—an artifact trail—of how to get to the future we envision. By simply mapping out the series of small, tangible steps on the way to the final outcome, the artifact trail helps people start taking action. Just like the map in the World War I story, the trail helps you move forward, even if the pathway isn't exactly right. But the artifact trail helps you to know which direction you should be heading, what we call your *vector of search*, to accompany your vision and gives you the insight into the next step you can take today. Although the trail is seldom completely correct and needs updating as you go along, it gives you an idea of what to do today to start creating the future.

To create an artifact trail from the strategic narrative you developed earlier as the north star, work backward to map out all the observable, tangible artifacts that can be created along the way to the end goal. In between the tangible artifacts, such as in-market proofs of concept, add the measurable outcomes and small wins that show progress. Examples include the establishment of the experiment team, commitment of uncommon partners, participation in a major conference, or agreement on a major issue. Tangible artifacts can be crude prototypes, physical objects, or even videos, but they must be observable. For example, the artifact trail for the AR and VR project portfolio included multiple experiences along the way. We launched each experience with a defined, limited period to force momentum toward iterating and improving for the next step.

The simplified version of our artifact trail describes only the major steps (figure 4-3). Within each step, there were multiple smaller artifacts, experiments, and data-driven indicators. Before the Holoroom, we created the touchscreen on a rail and the iPad you could point at QR codes. We created these in six weeks to start learning and to demonstrate measurable progress. After these artifacts, we developed a second version of the iPad setup, which could measure the dimensions of the room, again in just a few weeks. We also created and launched videos, internally and externally, to show our progress. Each of these steps created learning events for us, helped reassure the organization that we were making progress, and began

FIGURE 4-3

Lowe's AR/VR artifact trail

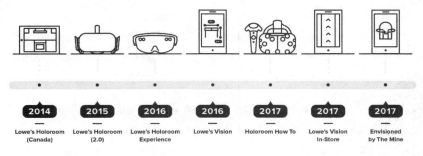

2014	2015	2016	2016	2017	2017	2017
Lowe's Holoroom (Canada)	Lowe's Holoroom (2.0)	Lowe's Holoroom Experience	Lowe's Vision	Holoroom How To	Lowe's Vision In-Store	Envisioned by The Mine

Source: Courtesy Uncommon Partners.

to engage customers and employees in our narrative vision. Thus, your artifact trail should include a good deal more than the simplified artifact trail depicted in the figure. It should include every small win, confidence creator, and data-driven indicator you can incorporate. The experimental design canvas described later in this chapter can help you create some of these points. But be creative in finding and incorporating authentic small wins.

How to Create an Artifact Trail

More than the simple trail depicted in figure 4-3, a working artifact trail will include the small steps that promote learning and confidence in the ultimately larger final outcome.

1. *Map out all the small steps leading to the final vision.*

   - Use the narrative as a north star for the end point, but don't re-create the story at every step. Instead, deconstruct the narrative by thinking through the steps required to reach that end state.

- Aim to create as many small, fast steps as possible. You need to show fast, early wins to make the story real and to maintain your own confidence and that of others.

- Focus on visible and tangible artifacts that you can start learning from and that are observable to skeptical outsiders. Sometimes, the artifacts may be "pretend-o-types" or virtual prototypes—drawings, renderings, or other visuals to help you start learning.

- Don't get caught in the trap of a long path to building a full, complicated solution before you can show success. You will likely fail if you do.

2. *Start prototyping using rigorous experimental design.* The later section on the experimental design canvas explains how you can use rigorous experimentation to obtain data on an initiative and determine its success.

   Know what to pivot on. You can change the artifacts and the story, but not the experimental design.

- Don't be afraid to pivot: modify or change the artifacts or even the story as you learn new information.

- Don't change rigorous experimental design—stick to your principles in conducting good experiments.

Caveats and Alternatives: No Plan Survives First Contact with Reality

Ultimately, the purpose of the artifact trail is to provide you with an initial map so that you can start taking action, to accelerate your learning, and to give the organization confidence that you are making progress (not just spending money on useless initiatives). Along the way, you should be learning, gathering new insights, and even encountering surprises that require you to change. No plan survives first contact with reality.[8] You should expect to pivot. Because of life's unpredictability, you should, somewhat counterintuitively, start small if you can, keeping the initiative under wraps until there is evidence—compelling data about the next direction to take, a market launch if it's a product, or an organizational scale-up if it's an initiative. By starting small and quietly, you can pivot more easily and save face doing so.

Admittedly you can't always start small with a major transformation, but with the small-then-large approach to transformation, you should first try, whenever possible, to gather the data showing that an approach works, before you announce the grand vision. As you gather this data, you will find you need to adapt as you go. But as you adapt, you may find that making adjustments with prototypes can be easier (since the prototype represents a vector of search within the vision) than changing the narrative (doing so may change the vision). Nonetheless, the vision must sometimes change and so must the narrative, which is the best tool for managing and communicating that vision. The following section, "Master Class: Modifying the Narrative When Something Big Changes," describes some steps you can take to alter your narrative.

Master Class: Modifying the Narrative When Something Big Changes

What should you do if something goes wrong along the artifact trail? It could be something within your domain of influence—a technology goes off the rails, a partner disappears, or customers just don't like what you are doing. It could also be something outside your control. Perhaps there is a massive change of direction in your organization, or maybe the whole sector changes in some fundamental way (think of the dot-com crash). As Garud, Schildt, and Lant explain, in any of these cases, you could make things much worse for yourself if you try to (1) scapegoat someone else, (2) blame external factors, (3) ignore the past, or (4) otherwise try to provide excuses. Doing so will only call into question your own competency.[9]

Instead, when something goes wrong, you can try one of two tactics. First, you can revisit the narrative, building on the past, but evolving it to take advantage of a different valuable future. For example, after Evan Williams discovered that Odeo, a podcasting platform, had limited appeal to users, the team repositioned the company to become Twitter. To do so, he and the others (including Jack Dorsey, who had the idea, and Noah Glass, who led the development of the solution) told a story about how Twitter enabled both listening and writing, but with much less effort because of the 140-character limit.[10]

Second, you may try redrawing the connections in your earlier story to new connections that allow you to go in a different direction. Specifically, you may need to cut ties with some symbols or organizations and create new ties with others. For example, after the dot-com bubble burst, many companies that had emphasized their internet capabilities dropped the dot-com appellation and then established connections to other legitimate industries like graphic design, advertising, and media. Similarly, in the 1980s, when AI failed to live up to expectations, many AI companies repositioned their capabilities as "natural language processing," "expert systems," or even "antivirus" software.[11]

As you retell your stories, you may find that stakeholders who felt threatened by the change of expectations may take a more micro-managing role in what you are doing. If you can redirect their energy into helping you frame the new narrative (e.g., "help me communicate what this could be"), then their involvement may build their and others' commitment to, rather than criticism of, your efforts.[12]

Tool: Experimental Design Canvas

Once you have an idea of which direction to go—your artifact trail—and of your initial steps, it's time to get serious about creating the metrics that can guide your search and create confidence among those around you. To generate these metrics, what we call the future KPIs (fKPIs), you can rely on experimental design, an overlooked superpower in the transformation toolkit, to deal with the fear of uncertainty. The experiment design canvas will help you design the metrics for success (figure 4-4). Although the experimental design canvas represents our approach to designing fKPIs, there are many appropriate approaches to experimental design. The key is to create meaningful, believable fKPIs, instead of targeting what is easy to test or using what we call mature metrics—metrics such as profit and market share that may be appropriate for measuring a mature business but totally inappropriate for measuring a new innovation or transformation initiative.

How to Use the Experimental Design Canvas

As a quick walkthrough, the strategic narrative and artifact trail provide the starting points for phase 1, which is to identify the narrative's *killer assumptions*—the big questions that, if proven false, will stop the initiative—that need to be tested. Your goal is not to identify every assumption but to identify the most important ones.

In phase 2, you turn these assumptions into testable hypotheses. A hypothesis is not a question, but a statement that is measurable and needs to be proven or disproven (that it can be proven or disproven is critical, and in the broader scientific community this crucial characteristic is called *falsifiability*). For example, if the killer assumption in Lowe's visualization had been "Will VR or AR help customers envision a remodel?" then one of many testable hypotheses could be the following: "If we depict a remodel in AR using a tablet, customers will be 50 percent more engaged or likely to commit to purchase."

The hypothesis gives you something to test and identifies the variables. In our work with Lowe's, the *dependent variable*, or outcome, is customer engagement or the increased likelihood of

FIGURE 4-4

Experimental design canvas

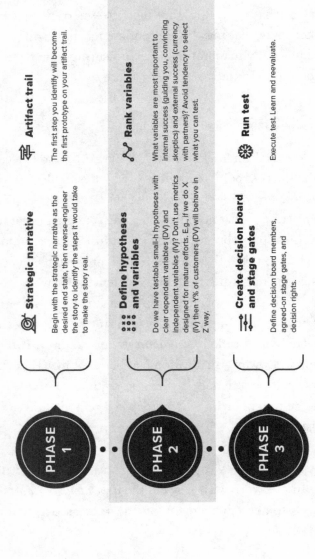

PHASE 1

🎯 **Strategic narrative**

Begin with the strategic narrative as the desired end state, then reverse-engineer the story to identify the steps it would take to make the story real.

⇄ **Artifact trail**

The first step you identify will become the first prototype on your artifact trail.

❓ **Killer assumptions**

Decide on big questions or assumptions in the strategic narrative that need testing. For example, will virtual reality (VR) or augmented reality (AR) help customers envision a remodel?

PHASE 2

⦂⦂ **Define hypotheses and variables**

Do we have testable small-h hypotheses with clear dependent variables (DV) and independent variables (IV)? Don't use metrics designed for mature efforts. E.g., If we do X (IV), then Y% of customers (DV) will behave in Z way.

⋏ **Rank variables**

What variables are most important to internal success (guiding you, convincing skeptics) and external success (currency with partners)? Avoid tendency to select what you can test.

⊕ **Define the experiment**

Decide on the time, location, scope, and controls. Look for mini-experiments.

PHASE 3

⇅ **Create decision board and stage gates**

Define decision board members, agreed-on stage gates, and decision rights.

✳ **Run test**

Execute test. Learn and reevaluate.

⟲ **Pivot and repeat**

What new direction do you need to go? Restart at phase 1, 2 or 3.

purchase, and the *independent variable*—the thing that causes the outcome—is depicting the remodel with the AR tablet. Alternatively, we could compare AR and VR as competing independent variables and hypothesize that "AR will lead to 20 percent greater customer engagement than will VR." Ultimately, you are creating measurable hypotheses because the quantification helps create meaningful measures to guide you. The difference between what you hypothesized and what happened is where the most valuable learning occurs.

In addition to defining the hypotheses, you will also want to define the variables, or what you measure and how you will measure it (in the example above, we define how we will measure engagement). Defining meaningful measures can create internal validity and external currency. Here you want to avoid simply testing what is easy to test, mainly because it leads to the tendency toward mature metrics, which can lead you to optimize for the wrong things too early. For example, if we focused on mature metrics, we could have tried to use AR to optimize sales in the short run, instead of focusing on the real customer problem (i.e., the challenge of envisioning a remodel). In doing so we could have gotten stuck optimizing an incremental improvement that solved our problem of near-term sales, but that didn't ultimately solve the customer problem and so missed the big opportunity: transforming how people envision their remodel.

Think carefully about the opportunities to define meaningful variables, ones that could create some internal and external currency. For example, we used applied neuroscience to measure engagement with VR and AR (we describe the measures later in the chapter). This brain research allowed us to see what no one else was seeing. With this knowledge, we created valid, comparable benchmarks that we could use with partners like Google and Microsoft as enticing reasons to offer us their best technology. Finally, you need to rank the variables to assess which are most important to achieve, and then focus on these. You can't do it all!

In phase 3, you define the experiment, namely, the time, location, control conditions, and scope. Control conditions are used in natural sciences and can be a control group that doesn't receive the treatment (they are the group to which nothing happens). There are also within-subject controls. For these controls, the same people participate in many experiments and each person, in a different experiment, effectively becomes his or her own control. For example, in the aforementioned light bulb redesign, we compared the regular store exhibit (the control group), the price redesign, and the bulb-type redesign. In the same way, we compared users exploring the VR or AR solutions and traditional in-store displays (the control group).

With the test defined, set up a decision board that has complete decision rights, and agree to employ stage gates, or stepwise sequences of decisions on whether to continue with a project. Because you are doing something new inside the organization, you want to move quickly to gather data, pivot when needed, and then start accumulating successes. Having to go through the traditional corporate hierarchy of steering committees will slow you down and lead the highest-paid people to distort your efforts. Instead, use the decision board to help you have honest discussions about what you are learning and what to do next. The board acts more like venture capitalists than like managers. Its goal is to guide you to your best outcome by seriously and honestly looking at the data rather than at the overly optimistic presentations you make when you are just trying to win a budget from a leader.

Generating fKPIs to Guide You through the Future

When we were creating prototypes at Lowe's, we faced a difficult choice determining how to scale visualization tools. We had prototyped visualization and home remodeling tools using more than five different augmented and virtual reality devices. In light of the customer and employee response, Lowe's was eager to scale the technology. Which one should it choose? The comic book depicted a customer wearing a virtual reality headset device. But when we attended a demonstration event for one of the major VR producers, we were a bit disturbed by a clue that no one seemed to notice: as a customer tried out the VR headset, exclaiming amazement, at the very same moment of expressing their excitement they often took off the headset. Although the eager engineers at the company developing the VR device didn't notice it, we did. Something else was going on.

In this case, you could use applied neuroscience to understand what is going on when people are wearing the VR headsets. You would observe that although it is exciting, their brains quickly became overloaded. And just as they crossed the critical overload threshold, they would take off the headset. So even though customers were telling engineers they loved it, their brains revealed that the VR experience was too much. By contrast, using applied neuroscience, you would observe that the smartphone-based AR allowed customers to lower the phone when their brains began to overheat; people could mentally cool down and then start over. This insight, only observable with experimental design and applied neuroscience, could guide your choices about which direction to go next . . . and it isn't always the sexiest technology.

Once you have defined some experiments, you need to design experimentation that will generate learning and other data that help you create the future. You can use many types of experiments, ranging from qualitative (i.e., not numerical) to quantitative. You can use familiar tools from qualitative research or marketing research, such as in-depth interviews, ethnographies, substitution studies, TURF studies (i.e., total unduplicated reach and frequency, a statistical tool used in marketing), and max-difference analysis. But as you use these tools, remember, your goal is not to generate statistical significance, but rather to produce the meaningful fKPIs you defined earlier. You want to create a process that leads to actions different than those that stymie most organizations. You are trying to create metrics that will help you see where to go and that will inspire those watching you to believe in your success (yes, as you have already seen, this point bears repeating).

Among the most promising tools for the experimental design of the future is applied neuroscience. This tool could overcome critical behavioral bottlenecks because it quantifies reactions that are inherently qualitative. Below we describe in detail how we have used applied neuroscience, a tool that is now much less expensive than you might think. But we also use other research tools, such as in-depth interviews (e.g., to figure out the organizational nomenclature and understand individual archetypes, as described earlier) and forced-choice experiments. We'll briefly describe how we have used a few of these alternatives, but a detailed discussion of these methods lies outside the scope of this book and can be found in many research-methods handbooks.

Tool: Applied Neuroscience

The XPRIZE Foundation is a privately funded organization awarding $20 million–$30 million prizes that address critical problems not receiving sufficient private or public attention (arguably, the commercial space industry, including SpaceX, came from XPRIZE awards). To define new prizes, XPRIZE brings together the XPRIZE Innovation Board, individuals such as Richard Branson, Will.i.am, Tony Robbins, and Peter Diamandis, at the Visioneers event to hear pitches and to vote for the project that could have the greatest impact.

When we attended the Visioneers event, one presentation stood out above the rest. An older Irish poet took the stage, journal in his left hand. He told how his craft had been words, building images like a contractor who builds with hammer and nails. But now Alzheimer's disease was taking away the thing he most loved, stealing the hammer from his toolbox and the nails while he slept. At times, he couldn't remember his son, and soon, he would completely forget all those he loved. As he described his loss, the room reverberated with sorrow and empathy for this man. Later, at the final awards ceremony, everyone clapped enthusiastically when the Alzheimer's challenge, led by Philip Edgcumbe (winner of the 2017 Canadian Medical Hall of Fame Award), became the next XPRIZE.

Although we celebrated as well, a more calculating skeptic might ask, Was it actually the best outcome, measured as impact on the largest group of people and likelihood to succeed? Arguably, some of the more cerebral projects, like clean air, zero-waste mining, or cybersecurity, could affect hundreds of millions of people, all of whom were suffering. But these more intellectual projects didn't have a chance compared with the emotion of the Alzheimer's presentation. For the more plain projects, competing against the Alzheimer's project was like bringing a bicycle to a motorcycle race. Although none of the attendees could really articulate it, other than saying that the Alzheimer's project really "connected," we could see the connection because we were using applied neuroscience tools to study volunteers, who wore EEG headsets throughout sessions. Moreover, with the applied neuroscience tools, we could also see that it wasn't just the emotion or the stories presenters told that held the judges. We found that the way the other potential participants had presented the data, the length of the evaluation form, the comfort of the chairs, and even the lighting in the room was biasing the ratings downward for the other potential prizes. With data that used people's brain patterns (six million data points per person) to measure when and how they reacted, we understood precisely the factors shaping decisions and which ideas were just a little too new or unfamiliar to the audience. Using this big data, the XPRIZE Foundation has the opportunity to reshape the system and even the playing field so that the huge amounts of capital and power that have the potential to change the direction of science and benefit millions are allocated as fairly as possible.

We have used applied neuroscience tools to explore things as simple as rethinking price tags in Tesco stores and as radical as Facebook's VR strategy. Applied neuroscience provides a scientific basis for defining and measure things like creativity, passion, and decision making. This research tool can also be used to develop indicators that allow you to neuroprototype any initiative, to uncover what no consultant, consumer, or stakeholder can tell you directly—what he or she is most likely to accept and adopt. The brain-based indicators generated from neuroprototyping provide critical feedback and signposts to guide you through the inevitable wilderness accompanying truly long leaps.

As just mentioned, neuroprototyping allows you to understand what no users can tell you outright. For example, many years ago, Greg Berns, a scholar at Emory University, performed several neuroscience studies of how teenagers responded to new and unknown music on Myspace. More recently, while watching the Super Bowl, Burns sat up straight during one of the ads: he recognized some of the music from his Myspace music study several years earlier. Curious, he reexamined the data. He found that when he measured what people said they liked about the unfamiliar music, it had no correlation with which music actually became popular. But if he measured the "wanting" responses when people listened to the music (in a deep brain structure called the nucleus accumbens) using neuroscience tools, he could predict with surprising success which music would become popular.[13]

Other researchers have now shown the same to be true of other unknowns. For example, although people's self-reported reactions to new movie trailers provide almost no indication of whether the movie will succeed, their brain's reactions (whenever the frontal parts of the brain have higher beta-frequency activation) prove incredibly predictive of box-office sales.[14]

As it turns out, we have separate systems for wanting and liking, and the deeper, less conscious wanting system seems to predict what we will act on and actually choose before we know it ourselves. What we consciously like seems to occur at a later stage in the brain. For example, researchers at Brian Knutson's lab at Stanford University used fMRI to demonstrate that brain reactions to different products can predict people's product choices as much as eight to twelve seconds before they know what choice they will make themselves.[15] Moreover, these predictions hold even when the researchers are testing small groups of people. Researchers at Lucas Parra's lab at the City University of New York found that using just a small group, around sixteen people, they could predict Nielsen ratings and Twitter reactions for popular television shows with the same accuracy as if they tested thousands of people.[16] Humans appear to have a highly common response to certain events—a commonality that predicts how we will like cultural goods.

In short, we love applied neuroscience because it can provide tools to cut through the misinformation of what people say (or can't say) to understand what really motivates them. (For more detail about what neuroscience is and what we measure, see the sidebar "What Is Applied Neuroscience Exactly?") Neuroscience can diagnose where and when biases occur, explain why they occur, and predict where to go next. Like in the AR and VR example, it can help you see what users are likely to adopt now, what they may adopt in a few years, and what they will never adopt. It also provides insight into how those you lead are reacting to your narrative and how to overcome the hurdles they won't speak about. In some ways, neuroscience provides a sort of crystal ball. Of course, your views of probabilities evolve over time, as people get used to new technologies or changes. But applied neuroscience can provide a data-driven map to navigate the future. You can use applied neuroscience in two primary ways—when you and your stakeholders are defining problems and when you are finding solutions for the users.

What Is Applied Neuroscience Exactly?

Applied neuroscience is the application of neuroscience tools and in-sights to measure and understand human behavior. Applied neuro-science typically uses a large, stationary fMRI (functional magnetic resonance imaging) or EEG (electroencephalograph) headsets and eye trackers to get a precise understanding of how the human brain re-acts to innovations, products, or other initiatives. We prefer using high-resolution EEG headsets and eye trackers because they are low-profile (people feel as if they are wearing a baseball cap and often forget about the gear) and portable (so you can wander around a rap battle or a retail store equally easily). These research-quality tools, not to be con-fused with low-quality consumer devices, generate massive amounts of data allowing the observation of multiple dimensions of brain activ-ity that affect decision making. Although we discuss measures that can be developed through applied neuroscience, this field of science is not merely a measurement stick. Applied neuroscience is a profound new way of understanding and transforming human thought and action. We have developed measures from the research in this larger field, but these measures should be taken in the context of psychology, neuro-science, and economics.

Using applied neuroscience, Thomas has developed a set of open, scientifically validated measures. *Scientifically validated* means they are grounded in peer-reviewed research, and *open* means they have been published so that other scientists can see these measures and evalu-ate them. (Beware of providers who won't reveal the science or met-rics behind what they are doing under the guise of IP rights. Such black-box solutions are unnecessary, as the required brain science is already well known and documented.)

We typically select four measures to assess what is working:

- *Cognitive load:* Are people understanding, bored, or over-loaded with information?

- *Motivation:* Are people stimulated to take action, neutral, or actively deterred?

- *Emotional arousal:* Are people emotionally engaged or disengaged?

- *Attention:* What are people focusing on? What is the stopping power of an item or information, and how good is it at holding on to attention?

These four measures give us a picture of what is working and not working. Often we will summarize these measures in charts (figure 4-5). For example, the left-hand chart in the figure plots emotional arousal against motivation. The upper left area indicates avoidance; the lower left, dislike; the lower right, interest (but not enough to produce action);

FIGURE 4-5

The relationship between emotional arousal or cognitive load and motivation

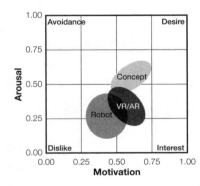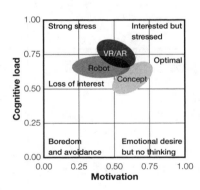

Source: Courtesy Neurons Inc.

Note: The emotion plot (at left) describes two dimensions of emotional responses. Arousal (Y-axis) denotes the intensity of an emotion, while motivation (X-axis) indicates the valence of the emotion, as approach or avoidance behavior. This plot provides insight into unconscious evaluations and potential avenues for optimizing emotional responses. The thinking-versus-feeling plot (at right) illustrates the intensity of cognitive and emotional responses. Here, cognitive load (Y-axis) shows the amount of information that is being processed, while motivation (X-axis) indicates emotional valence, as approach or avoidance behavior. This plot reveals the relative weight of emotional and cognitive responses. The shaded areas indicate the typical range of scores for different types of inventions. VR = virtual reality; AR = augmented reality.

and the upper right, desire that leads to action. Typically the relationship between useful motivation and emotional arousal is not linear. The most advantageous emotional response (desire) results from high motivation and high arousal, whereas the least helpful emotion (avoidance) comes from low motivation and high arousal, not low arousal. Arousal exacerbates the effects of motivation, leading emotional responses to have a U-shaped pattern. The strongest emotional responses occur when arousal is at its maximum.

Similarly, the right-handed chart compares cognitive load against motivation. This chart plots the ideal zone of cognitive load that is associated with motivated action, as opposed to overload or boredom. Here, an optimal score occurs when people are motivated and show a moderately high cognitive load, which is a signal that there is both interest and comprehension of whatever is being processed.

Together these measures help show how users or stakeholders react to an idea or a solution, not just in aggregate, but also literally at every millisecond. This precision allows you to pinpoint exactly what is not working, so you can avoid it, and what is working, so you can amplify it.

Neuroprototyping the Problem with Leaders and Stakeholders

Although we often start developing the strategic narrative and discovering bottlenecks with in-depth interviews, we also conduct neuroscientific research on the narratives themselves. We use applied neuroscience to see where the story might be creating resistance (so that we can resolve it) and where the story is working well (so that we can amplify it). We've tested many stories across various media, from comic books to interactive digital tools to videos and even to live speaking engagements like XPRIZE, and we have found some interesting points about how the brain reacts to story.

Comic books, with their unique mix of engaging visuals, compelling story, and focused reading, proved to be some of the strongest tools for keeping readers in that cognitive sweet spot throughout the story. But the content and style make a big difference. For example, simple stories are the most successful at delivering a message, but they may fall short of helping the reader understand the technology being communicated. Artwork that feels dark and ominous may start to lead to some negative reactions to the readers. Negative reactions may sometimes be the goal, but you need to understand this potential downside as you create the story.

You can see some of these insights come to life in real time if you equip the comic-book readers with neuro equipment and observe their responses. The results can make for some important real-time dialogue about what's working or not working in the story. Using applied neuroscience, we've spotted problems that internal stakeholders have had with some stories, and we've had a conversation with these stakeholders before the issue gets too far down the road. For the best understanding, however, you need to gather a full data set and complete an analysis (usually requiring just a few weeks) that can help you adjust the story before it is shared further or optimize future stories. In the XPRIZE example, imagine if at future Visioneers events, we could pretest presentations and help coach presentation teams to adjust their style or content based on what audience members can't fully express.

Neuroprototyping the Solution with Users

Henry Ford supposedly said, "If I had asked people what they wanted, they would have said faster horses." However, if it had been available, he probably could have used applied neuroscience to figure out what they really wanted. Neuroprototyping can provide evidence-based signposts to guide the development of solutions, particularly for radical ideas where customers struggle to express their deeper emotions. For example, when we have tested technologies like robots, we find idiosyncrasies, such as how people like robots more when the machines are programmed to make mistakes, such as bump into things or stop momentarily. Few customers can overtly tell you such things, although they might laugh when the robot makes a mistake.[17] But after observing people's brain activity, you can see that such things decrease people's fear of a new technology and make it more approachable. Similarly, although it may make intuitive sense to add more features to technologies like virtual reality or robots, for example, allowing customers to connect to a staff member for live video chat or creating more controls in a virtual reality world, counterintuitively customers often find such features overwhelming and too disruptive.

Whether you are creating new products, business models, or initiatives, neuroprototyping can provide predictive, evidence-based feedback about the path with the highest probability of success. We suggest how you can access these tools (they are relatively inexpensive) in "Digital Toolbox: How to Access Applied Neuroscience" as well as how you can use some rough alternatives if you can't get access to these tools yourself.

Master Class: Other Ways to Apply Experimental Design to the Future

Although we have described applied neuroscience as our preferred method for creating metrics to guide you through the future, not everyone can easily access applied neuroscience (see "Digital Toolbox: How to Access Applied Neuroscience" in this chapter). Fortunately, there are many experimental design tools that don't require neuroscience that are both common and inexpensive. These tools may lack the power to uncover the exact mechanisms or to separate the rational from the emotional elements of human response, but they are still worthwhile. We already mentioned several of these tools, such as in-depth interviews, ethnographies, substitution studies, TURF studies, and max-difference studies. Let's look at a few examples.

Sometimes, qualitative tools like in-depth interviews can go a long way in resolving key issues before you design a rigorous experiment. We were once part of an investment team for a disruptive new microscope (orders of magnitude improvement in magnification and decrease of cost). We wanted to learn if university researchers would want to use and buy the microscope, so we contacted professors and asked for some time to speak. We had assembled a semistructured interview guide (how to do this is widely available online and in research-methods books) to explore our key hypotheses about professors' needs, their flexibility in their research agenda, their evaluation processes for buying new microscopes, funding and purchasing cycles, and so forth.

We learned a great deal about each of these elements from the interviews, but what surprised us most was their answer to how they evaluated these new microscopes. They told us that they had never heard of this type of microscope before, and so they had consulted the head of the university imaging lab to find out more. Pause for a moment. The professors we spoke with revealed something profound: rather than searching on Google or asking a colleague, they went to the head of the imaging lab. This response told us something critical about whom we needed to be working with. This technology was probably just too new for professors deeply embedded in their existing research agendas. Rather, the point of adoption would most likely be the people in charge of exploring and adopting new technologies—the head of the university imaging lab! Of course, we later interviewed these people as well and learned much about how to make this technology successful.

For another alternative, we have used inexpensive implicit association tests (IATs) to draw out unconscious reactions when applied neuroscience was out of reach. Associations are heuristics for our minds to make fast judgments about our environment. For example, what do you think about when you see the brand name Volvo? Some associations may come to mind: car, driving, Swedish, safety. What about Ferrari? Maybe you think of fast, red, luxury, but probably not safety. These associations have been shaped by decades of branding. But what do you associate when a name is made up? What do you think of when you read "Koprak" or "Oalimo"? Try saying these names aloud or in your head. Now ask yourself, which one has a logo with sharp edges? Which one has a logo with rounded edges? Which brand comes from Eastern Europe, and which from Spain or Portugal? Most people associate Koprak with a sharp logo and place it in Eastern Europe, and they associate Oalimo with a round logo and something from Spain, Portugal, or the United States. What makes these associations interesting is the connections we make even when no such thing exists at all.

Understanding how our brains make these associations provides a complementary set of tools, or an alternative, to the applied neuroscience tools we have described. An IAT provides one way to use the brain's functionality to conduct an experiment to reveal people's subconscious reactions. There are different types of IATs, but one of the primary approaches can be applied as follows:

1. Ask participants to rate words as either positive or negative.

2. Select words that you are interested in having tested (e.g., positive and negative words related to your project, idea, or brand).

3. Select other filler words, as well as a list of projects, ideas, or brands.

4. Use suitable software to present each word randomly and rapidly, and record the accuracy and speed of the responses to each word.

5. Between each word, present a brand name, a logo, or other relevant items, and ensure that you record the responses to each subsequent word.

At the core, the idea behind the IAT is that the brand can affect the accuracy and especially the response time to the word being presented after the brand. We use the word *brand* because that is the original application of the test, but the test can be applied more broadly to uncover the subconscious reactions to a concept, product, or change. If a participant loves the brand you show, then the person is more likely to correctly identify the word as a positive word, and with a faster response. If the participant hates the brand, he or she may make more errors and the response time will be slower. The opposite happens for negative words.

The mechanism of the test is relatively simple: when we see something (image, brand, or product) that we like, we get in a positive emotional microstate, and if the next item is negative for us, we need time to readjust away from the positive microstate. This disconnect creates a small but measurable lag in response time. Similarly, if we dislike the preceding image, then it's much easier to categorize the next negative word right afterward—no need to readjust the emotional microstate.

By measuring the relative response time (and accuracy) to word or images, you can infer which associations are most connected to a project, a brand, or an idea. In this way, you can map out the different associations to a brand, a product name, or other aspects, such as a product or concept, as shown in the spider plots in figure 4-6.

As you can see, associations with Volvo and Ferrari are quite different. The same test can be run with new names or services. In fact, numerous studies have demonstrated that the IAT can measure implicit biases such as political preferences, implicit racism, brand preferences, and partnership preferences.[18]

The IAT, when performed correctly, can provide powerful insights into subconscious and direct associations. While the IAT can be done in a central location, online solutions are also available. Online survey tools that incorporate the IAT, like Qualtrics, make using the IAT scalable, increasing result validity. We have applied IATs for creative services (e.g., Lowe's Holoroom), new business models (e.g., IKEA), innovative concepts (e.g., architectural living

FIGURE 4-6

Brand associations: Ferrari versus Volvo

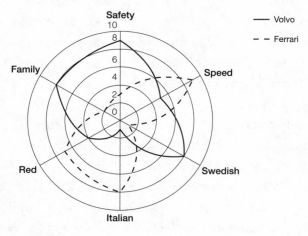

Source: Courtesy Neurons Inc.

spaces for Emirati holding company Majid Al Futtaim), and new products (e.g., for a global food company), so the tool is versatile.

Tool: Behavioral Database

Finally, if the goal of experimental design is to create the KPIs to guide the future, don't overlook the power of a behavioral database to optimize your decisions. Such a database captures information that can be used to understand the relationships between the data from your experiments and the customer behavior you are looking to optimize (e.g., adoption of the technology). It can consist of qualitative or quantitative data (or both) and can be used to amplify the value of your fKPIs, save time in the experimentation process, or reveal new insights. Although the term *behavioral database* might sound intimidating, you can build one yourself or access a database using free or nearly free tools. If you can use Excel, you can use a

How to Access Applied Neuroscience

Applied neuroscience tools are probably best obtained through a third-party provider—it will be cheaper and faster until you can build your own capability (if you so choose). With full disclosure, we suggest Neurons, which Thomas founded, as one of the best choices. Thomas created Neurons specifically to do this work and to base it on the most rigorous, open, and reliable neuroscience. He has also created several online digital tools that can be accessed instantly. Another of Thomas's projects in progress is Neurons in a Box, a solution you can use to start neuroprototyping on your own without having to involve Neurons extensively. There are other providers out there, but we advise you to be sure to assess the openness and validity of the science behind what they are doing. For more on the potential issues, go to https://brainethics.wordpress.com. There, Thomas discusses his original concerns with some unethical practices—concerns that led him to found Neurons in the first place.

behavioral database. And these days, you can probably use another scary word—machine learning—to understand the world in surprising ways.

To create your own behavioral database, simply feed the data from your experiments into a searchable, aggregated database that you can then manipulate to understand what variables optimize a desired outcome. For example, as described in chapter 3, when Kate worked at a major food retailer, there was a big mystery about massive overstocks of oranges. Kate used free Google Trends search data to discover what an entire team had overlooked—the extended flu seasons that had led growers and retail executives to misperceive a short-term trend as a long-term trend. Similarly, Kate used the company's data to spot high-trial, low-repeat items and low-trial, high-repeat items to capture millions in missed sales. Likewise, when we created a behavioral database at Lowe's using results from all our studies, we began to spot insights across studies.

Using neuroprototyping can be one way to build a behavioral database. In many ways, applied neuroscience could be described as the generation of big data to understand the human mind. For example, a typical study with thirty participants will generate three billion data points from the EEG and ten million data points from eye tracking. This kind of data allows the visualization of precisely when and how decisions are being made—information with potentially immense predictive power. If you capture this data efficiently, you can reuse it and go on a digital walk-along with customers during and after their experience, so that you can uncover their reactions. Linking that neural data to behavioral outcomes like purchase decisions makes the data even more valuable. Your primary behavioral database could simply be all the neuroprototyping data you gathered, tied to specific outcomes, such as engagement with a technology, liking a technology, purchasing a product, or spending money.

You develop a behavioral database as you would your fKPIs: focus on the real behavior that matters. Too often, big companies focus on longitudinal data (data collected over time) only loosely linked to the key behavior they want. For example, many companies overemphasize net promoter score (a measure that has received significant criticism recently), assuming that it drives customer loyalty, which drives purchasing behavior. But are those the real drivers that lead to purchasing? In asking the question, we aren't joining the critics skeptical of net promoter scores. Rather, we are asking which direct behaviors you want to measure and observe. And then, if possible, you should be creative in generating a database that allows you to understand the levers directly driving those behaviors. For example, in the B2B realm, global maritime company DNV GL aggregated the disparate data sources in aquaculture (or fish farming) to create a behavioral database. First, it pulled together data from the fish farmers on pen location; pen size; fish count; and feeding times, amounts, and patterns. It then combined that data with nutritional data from feed producers and public data on weather, tides, temperatures, and so forth. In this way, DNV GL created a valuable, detailed picture of behaviors to dramatically improve the variables that matter most to fish farmers: more fish at lower cost.

How to Use a Behavioral Database

A behavior database can provide information to help you make the right decisions about your organization's future. Follow these steps to get started.

1. *Find or start building a behavioral database.*

   - Start capturing data from all of your experiments.

   - Combine that data with free data (as in the fish farming example above) or other data inside your organization.

   - Try to capture as directly as possible any data related to the behaviors you want to optimize.

2. *Analyze the data.* Find a way to explore the data, learn from it, and optimize critical outcomes.

   - Don't be afraid of data analysis. Machine learning today is as easy as learning Excel. Machine learning simply means letting the software look for patterns in the data.

   - Do access free or nearly free tools, like TensorFlow—a free machine-learning algorithm you can learn in just over an hour. Use it to explore the data.

   - Don't let data override your common sense. Data mining can lead to false correlations. You are still the expert running the machine.

3. *Become a behavioral database ninja.* As you grow more familiar with the tool, you will develop more and more expertise.

- Ensure that you are measuring what you claim you are.

- Use traceable IDs for better cross-source comparisons.

- Use a platform that allows large data sets and has a good solution for categorizing and searching data.

- Distinguish between database building and longitudinal additions to the database—at what stage are you?

- Be sure to set up protocols for adding data over time. Consistency is critical in setting up a behavioral database.

- Log all entries, additions, and changes to the database.

- Consider the types of analyses you want to do as part of the way you set up the database.

There are several ways to obtain databases; see "Digital Toolbox: Free or Nearly Free Tools to Access a Behavioral Database" for some suggestions.

Summary

In this chapter, we highlighted the fear of the unknown as a primary impediment to transformational change. When we enter the unknown, there are often few data points to guide us. To overcome the fear that holds us back, we must make the transformation as tangible as possible. To do this, we need to make real progress and accumulate small wins. The *artifact trail* can help us identify and execute on the opportunities for making the transformation tangible. But we also need to design the fKPIs, using an *experimental design canvas* that can guide our own steps and create the confidence that we are making progress. To generate these important

Free or Nearly Free Tools to Access a Behavioral Database

Most big organizations have data already. Find it, and start learning from it. There is also an incredible amount of free data and free tools online. Google AdWords Keyword Planner and Google Trends are hyperrapid ways to understand behaviors. For example, a quick Google Trends search for "digital transformation" reveals a steadily rising interest over the last three years, particularly in Europe and Australia, which peaks around conference season and dies during the December holidays. Similarly, TensorFlow, or related tools like Weka or BigML, may be the most brilliant and unbelievably simple way that anyone can apply machine learning to data. Online, we are building a repertoire of other free tools you can access, but Data.gov, European Union Open Data Portal, or Google Public Data Explorer are great places to start.

metrics, you can use many *experimental design* tools to create your future, but our favorite tools are supplied by *applied neuroscience*, which has special power to reveal the real mechanisms leading to change. Finally, linking the results of your experimental design to a *behavioral database* can give you greater insight into what drives behavior and can create shortcuts to insight in future work.

The available experimentation tools presented in this chapter are by no means comprehensive. Decades of work by inductive and deductive scientists inside and outside management have generated a wealth of available experimentation tools and procedures. But we rarely use these tools properly or effectively in big organizations. However, these tools and the others we describe offer some of the best, most reliable ways of providing confidence that we should persevere in creating the future.

FIVE

Leading the Self-Transforming Organization

Although Steve Jobs was famous for showing up on stage, casually dressed in a black turtleneck and jeans, to announce a radical new technology, his act wasn't entirely original. Edwin Land, most famous for inventing the instant camera a generation before Jobs, also showed up at annual events casually dressed (for the era), next to a midcentury Saarinen table, to announce revolutionary technology.[1] Jobs told interviewers that Land was "one of the great inventors of our time" and "a national treasure" and sought to imitate him, even down to the Saarinen-style table.[2] But despite Land's many inventions and his company's success in attracting some of the world's best scientists—Massachusetts Institute of Technology (MIT) and Harvard graduates who transformed the science of photography—the company still failed to leap into the digital future.

Although Polaroid, and its competitor Kodak, are often used as cautionary tales about the dangers of technology disruption, it wasn't the technology that killed these companies. Kodak actually invented the first digital camera in 1975 and, in 1989, invented a digital single-lens reflex (SLR) camera similar to models available on the market today. But both times, executives shut the projects down, arguing in 1975 that "no one would ever want to look at their pictures on a television set" and, later, that the digital SLR would cannibalize their film sales.[3] Similarly, just at the start of the digital-imaging revolution, Polaroid created some of the world's leading digital-imaging capabilities. Had Polaroid commercialized the camera they created, it would have been best in class. But instead, the company decided to focus on the film business because it was so profitable, and so Polaroid put those capabilities on the shelf until it was too late.[4]

As highlighted by these iconic failures, technology was not the reason these organizations failed to transform. Instead, the real challenge was people—helping people believe enough to commit to a future different from the familiar and then persisting through the disillusionment that precedes any change. Although we all recognize these challenges intuitively, we need better tools to address the true limitations. In this book, we have shared a process and some tools designed to address these behavioral limitations—the incrementalism, habit, and fear—that hold us all back.

But we have also emphasized that sometimes, the most successful transformations begin small and end big: small-t transformations that could add up to a big-T transformation. In this approach, each small project represents a moment of transformation. Each successful project helps the organization self-correct from the dead-end tendency in all organizations—to become a calcified machine executing a routine—to what they need to become to survive in the future: a malleable team capable of capturing new opportunities. Thus, one of the key challenges will be to find the small-t opportunities that can add up to a big-T transformation. Sometimes, however, circumstances demand starting with a big-T transformation—a global transformation immediately. We would argue that the process still applies—creating a strategic narrative, breaking bottlenecks, and then designing the KPIs to create the future. Even then, you would be wise to take a data-first approach rather than announcing a grand transformation that will make it hard to pivot and change.

Regardless of your path on your transformation journey, we highlight some critical capabilities to help you on your way. Specifically we describe the roles of negative capability, inverted power, chaos pilots, accelerator skill sets, uncommon partners, results first, the three noes, and yea-sayers.

Negative Capability

Today we know Richard Feynman as one of the legends of physics, one of the fathers of quantum mechanics, and winner of the Nobel prize, in part for his work on the wobble of electrons in orbit. But when a much younger Feynman joined the faculty of Cornell after the end of World War II, he didn't feel like the kind of scientist who would have such a significant impact on the direction of physics. Instead, he arrived physically and emotionally burnt out from the effort at Los Alamos to develop nuclear technologies, from the death of his wife, and from the task of creating new physics courses that had never been taught.

At the time he didn't recognize his own exhaustion and instead criticized himself incessantly for his inability to do what many see as the most important job of a professor—research. In his biography, Feynman describes feeling terrible for his lack of productivity for what felt like years.[5] Because he was in a new and emerging field, despite the lack of productivity, Feynman began to receive job offers from prestigious universities, as well as the Institute for Advanced Studies, the premier research institution for theoretical physics populated with legends like Einstein and von Neumann. But the offers only further compounded Feynman's self-doubt since he knew how unproductive he was in research.

Finally, one day, after months of self-torture, Feynman decided that he would give up trying to do important research and just let himself follow his own curiosity. In the past he had always let himself explore how the world worked, even if it was already known. For example, he was curious about the flow of water out of a faucet and let himself calculate the underlying physics of how water narrows as it flows out of a faucet. Feynman decided he would forget about research and just let himself explore.

A few days later, Feynman was sitting in the dining hall at Cornell when someone took one of the dining hall plates and tossed it in the air. He recalls noticing that the plate wobbled in the air as it spun but that the Cornell medallion in the center of the plate spun faster than the wobble. Feynman decided to see if he could calculate the difference between the speeds and describe it with an equation and then, getting more curious, if he could calculate the underlying physics (mass, acceleration, etc.) behind it. Soon Feynman had it solved and ran to his department chair (and legendary physicist), Hans Bethe, and described his formula. Bethe congratulated him but said, "Feynman, that's pretty interesting, but what's the importance of it?"

Feynman defiantly replied, "Hah! . . . There's no importance whatsoever. I'm just doing it for the fun of it." Looking back on that moment, Feynman recalls: "His reaction didn't discourage me; I had made up my mind I was going to enjoy physics and do whatever I liked." Feynman continued to work on the wobbles, which he described as play, and effortless, but totally unimportant, except that one insight led to another; those connections led to how electrons move in orbit and to key ideas in thermodynamics and quantum dynamics and eventually straight into the ideas for which he won the Nobel Prize. As Feynman later stated, "The diagrams and the whole business that I got the Nobel Prize for came from that piddling around with the wobbling plate."

Feynman's willingness to suspend judgement about the end result and instead entertain an idea to see where it leads illustrates an important capability for innovation and transformation: negative capability. The term *negative capability* was coined by the romantic poet John Keats, when he was describing writers like Shakespeare or other people "capable of being in uncertainties, mysteries, doubts, without any irritable reaching after fact & reason."[6] He was describing the capability to accept not having the answer immediately, but to explore how something may evolve.

In the modern context, negative capability could be thought of as the ability to be comfortable with uncertainty, even to entertain it, rather than to become so anxious by its presence that you have to prematurely race to a potentially more certain, but more likely suboptimal, conclusion. To be a visionary—to take giant leaps—you need to develop this negative capability. Whereas many people cannot stand the fuzziness of uncertainty, leaders of innovation and transformation frequently demonstrate negative capabilities. The negative capabilities facilitate the exploration of new terrain and the discovery of the adjacent possible.[7]

Inverted Power

Most of the time when we teach transformation or innovation inside established companies, people dismiss the idea as impossible unless it comes from the CEO. (Even in profitable, successful companies like IBM, Amazon, Apple, 3M, Intuit, ING, and Mastercard, people dismiss innovative transformation as impossible.) When Kyle started the innovation transformation at Lowe's, he was about as low power as you can imagine: a junior manager in the international research group. In other words, he started at the bottom of the pecking order.

Despite his lowly status, Kyle chose to see if he could ignite a transformation from within. Truthfully, he was helped at different points by leaders inside Lowe's—people able to envision possibilities and with the negative capability to endure the uncertainty while it emerged. But it wasn't an easy path at all. Kyle was challenged by skeptics inside and outside the company. During these periods, Kyle felt about one inch tall. Yet there were times when other leaders supported him and said things like, "This is exactly the kind of thing we need to be doing to transform this company."

Don't assume you have to be high power to start a transformation in your company. Many of the other transformations we have worked on have started at the lower ranks. Of course, if you start from the bottom, a transformation will take time. You will still need to seek support as high up in the organization as possible—we aren't saying you can do it alone. But inverted power—the power of leading from the bottom up—does work. Moreover, whether you are leading from the bottom or the top, it will still be difficult. A transformation challenges many of the behavioral tendencies that hold us back, and there is almost always resistance. This resistance will likely be greater the first time you start to effect a change. Like an old piece of machinery being roused from the field, where it has rusted for decades, the organization has to start reusing muscles it has not exercised for decades. But it becomes easier. At Lowe's, the AR and VR project was orders of magnitude harder to get started than were the later projects, like the exosuits.

Finally, don't assume that you need to have a massive budget. When Kyle started at Lowe's, he had a very small budget. You could begin with relatively little funding—it costs less than you think for stories, comics, applied neuroscience or other research techniques, and even technology to start building. Depending on what you already have on hand or what you can beg, borrow, or steal, you can start working right away. Be scrappy. The lower the cost, the lower the expectations for returns and the greater the glory for the results you do show.

Chaos Pilots

In 1991, Uffe Elbæk took out a $100,000 personal loan and opened a most unusual business school. To most lenders, the school would seem a very risky investment. Elbæk's previous experience had been the creation of the Frontrunners program, a Danish social experiment to counsel problem children. As part of his counseling work, Elbæk convinced the children to become street performers, and in the process, he created a transformative experience: instead of being looked down on as dropouts, the children were applauded for their performances and had their self-confidence restored. Eventually, Elbæk's program expanded to reach 250 troubled youth and then transformed into Aarhus Festival, Scandinavia's largest annual cultural program. While creating the program, Elbæk learned the skills to creatively navigate thorny, uncertain problems, a skill set he believed was urgently needed by the larger business world facing an increasingly turbulent environment. With the vision to teach the business world the skills to navigate uncertain problems, he founded Kaospilot, a hybrid of design school, business school, and personal development program. Although today Elbæk has moved on into politics, Kaospilot continues, led by Christer Windeløv-Lidzélius. The school has been so popular that it has spread across Scandinavia and the rest of Europe.[8]

In a recent TEDx talk, Windeløv-Lidzélius and David Storkholm describe their vision of Kaospilot students as embodying three characteristics: (1) the willingness to meet ideas, questions, and people openly and creatively; (2) the capability to work in teams with persistence, productivity, and passion; and (3) the capability to deliver results that have a positive impact on the team, the target group, and the greater community. To illustrate, Storkholm tells the story of a group of five female students who went to Sarajevo, Bosnia, and Herzegovina, shortly after the devastating civil war, to study urban development. When the students arrived, they discovered a depressed city from which talent had fled and where the remaining people felt they had little voice.

The Kaospilot team came up with a project—they invited six hundred young people to fill a 5,000-square-foot canvas with their dreams for Sarajevo. The team then wrapped the canvas around the historic youth center, creating a visual image of the hopes of the youth for their city. Later, the students took the artwork to Oslo, Norway, where designers transformed it into products—T-shirts, handbags, posters, etc.—which were then sold and the proceeds taken back to renovate the very same historic youth center. Storkholm emphasizes that the project produced results for the students (they found a creative way to study urban development), the target group (the youth felt that their voices had been heard), and the community (it gained renewed hope and funds to renovate).[9]

Although the Kaospilot school doesn't focus exclusively on transformation, the term *chaos pilot* is a perfect label for the kinds of people we are looking for when building a team. Chaos pilots are people who can creatively lead a project through uncertainty. They have negative capability, as we discussed, but they have other critical skills as well, such as how to structure chaos and take action regardless. But how do you find chaos pilots to join you? Besides the three characteristics Windeløv-Lidzélius and Storkholm described (openness to change, persistent teamwork, broad results), chaos pilots also care more about behavior change than about climbing the ladder or getting a star on their charts. They are more willing to be the nail that stands out or to ask a challenging question. Although it can sound romantic to be such a person, and many people believe they want to be so, being a chaos pilot is hard—you are working on projects that are ambiguous, and you are frequently getting beat up in the process. People who aren't capable of being chaos pilots quickly melt down.

Finding chaos pilots to join you can be challenging and is probably best done through observation and experimentation. Frankly, few people are born chaos pilots—most of us grow into the role. So the challenge is to find the people who can grow into the role and then to coach them. But there are a few fertile places to look for good candidates. For example, look for people getting mixed performance reviews but who are still highly prized by the organization. Often, these people are getting mixed reviews because they make those around them uncomfortable (because the potential candidates often challenge the status quo), but they don't get fired, because they perform so well. Typical reviews will read something like "doesn't know how to navigate the organization" or "not a team player," because these people are constantly challenging their bosses. But they are also so productive that they get comments like "super smart" or "gets an amazing amount done" and are consequently kept close to the heart of the organization.

As another character indicator, you might look for people who can handle criticism and disappointment. As a potential hypothesis, and at risk of over-generalizing cultural differences, perhaps one reason Kaospilot was founded in Denmark is that the Danes are great at complaining (or *brokke sig*, as it's called in Danish). You are less likely to find this same tendency in Sweden or Norway, which are otherwise culturally very similar. But in Denmark, *brokke sig* is acceptable and expected. Arguably, complaining creates an environment in which people are allowed to point out the flaws of something and even share their disappointment. Not surprisingly, many Danes are good at responding to criticism. So, just as the United States has embraced the Scandinavian term *hygge* in seeking inspiration for "coziness," perhaps we should be looking for the capacity to give, receive, and live with *brokke sig* when looking for chaos pilots.

Finally, you can also look for people who were placed into a project that changed dramatically along the way, but who navigated the change well or, even better, who rescued the project. You might also look for those who are willing to chase opportunities, regardless of prevailing wisdom about playing it safe. For example, people who ignored advice about risks to their careers and joined or led a particularly risky project may be good chaos pilot candidates. Finally, in assembling your team, you may also want to look for chaos survivors: they may not be the ones to lead through uncertainty like chaos pilots, but they bring the valuable skill of getting things done in a turbulent environment without having to be the one leading it.

Accelerator Skill Sets

During the early days of additive manufacturing, when everyone was racing to build desktop 3-D printers, we discovered something most people had overlooked—the real holdup to additive manufacturing was not the printers (which had been improving since the 1980s) but rather the 3-D imaging capabilities to bridge the divide between existing physical objects and 3-D printable objects. In response, during the early days of the project, Kyle struggled to find anyone who could create 3-D images that could then be printed. Eventually, he found a team of computer vision experts who agreed to form a startup to meet this challenge, but it was going to be a slow process and at great expense. Instead, Kyle recruited Mason Sheffield, a real-life MacGyver (a television hero who can build anything out of duct tape and a paper clip) who had previously been running development for *Call of Duty*.

When Mason found out about the quote, he laughed and then set to work. He didn't even have a proper office yet. Instead, working out of the offices above a Lowe's store in Seattle, he built a fully capable, 3-D scanning hardware and software device in four weeks for a fraction of the original cost estimate. Today, Lowe's has patented the system Mason built, and the company uses it to create incredibly detailed 3-D images. To get a sense of how detailed, consider the *Transformers* movie. Its Optimus Prime robot superhero was visualized with 1.8 billion polygons, whereas a Lowe's 3-D scan of a vase is 8 billion polygons (a polygon is a geometric object containing information about location, color, shading, and texture).

These 3-D images have proved incredibly powerful for online selling, increasing conversion for some items as much as 50 percent.[10] The multidimensional objects are also less expensive to create than traditional photos. To be fair, Mason had been focused on the 3-D facial-scanning feature for the *Call of Duty* game before he joined Kyle's group. But even with that background, Mason performed the impossible, soldering the hardware himself and coding the solution single-handedly. Later, he helped recruit the team to build the final answer to the 3-D content scanning challenge. Mason can only be described as having an accelerator skill set.

People with accelerator skill sets can catalyze your project, and they share the same vision that you have: to transform the organization. Sometimes, these skill sets are hardware or software related, but just as often, they just get things done or accelerate communication. For example, Amanda Manna, who joined Kyle early on at Lowe's, proved pivotal in managing the creation of narratives and in communicating externally. Manna's accelerator skills made the entire innovation lab at Lowe's much more successful. For example, Manna helped both to create the broader narrative capabilities inside Lowe's and to align the organization around those narratives (while also communicating those narratives externally). She also accelerated the scaling of these capabilities at Lowe's.

In assessing which accelerator skill sets you need, the key is to ask yourself what you are good at, what you are missing, and how you can assemble a team that has diverse backgrounds, thought, skill sets, and actions—but shared purpose and vision—so you can move quickly. Although accelerator skill sets are a specific recommendation, they are part of a larger transformational issue in organizations. When we talk about accelerator skill sets, we aren't just talking about cross-functional teams.

While ideas like cross-functional or complementarity are important first steps to breaking down silos, or inflexible, inefficient hierarchies in organizations, the terms mask a deeper problem at the heart of big organizations: the product/function organization structure. Most big companies are organized around products and functions, and although this structure works fine in a stable environment, this same structure creates problems when you want to start capturing opportunities that require the reorganization of capabilities.

By contrast, consider how startups organize themselves to do work. For example, there is a rule of thumb that if you want to create a software startup, you need a hustler, a hacker, and a hipster. Beneath the cute alliteration, the rule suggests that you will face three problems for which you need three matching capabilities: discovering the customer need (the hustler talks to customers), coding a solution (the hacker codes it), and the go-to-market strategy (the hipster optimizes the user interface to maximize customer acquisition).

Notice that the rule of thumb does not talk about creating cross-functional teams with sales, marketing, finance, and operations people led by a CEO. Instead, the general approach talks about the core problems the startup will face and the matching capabilities needed to solve those problems. Part of the reason startups often have an advantage over big companies (which already have money, people, industry knowledge, and distribution) is that the startups are faster at redeploying capabilities to match the evolving problems they face. And they are faster precisely because they employ a problem/capability structure instead of a product/function structure. Thus, acquiring accelerator skill sets doesn't mean getting someone really great from finance, strategy, and marketing. Instead, it means developing a team that allows you to quickly match problems to capabilities.

Uncommon Partners

In a dingy conference room at NASA, five prototypical nerds, smelling of Thai food, laid out the path to printing satellites in space and buildings on distant planets. At the end of their four-day marathon, they emerged with an artifact trail that began with early prototypes for the first 3-D printer on the International Space Station and ended in the additive-manufacturing future—a future much bigger than 3-D printing. In the additive-manufacturing future, we will view everything as transient, or capable of being repurposed into new things. Rather than throwing away a soda bottle or a bent nail, we will simply reprocess these things into a new hinge for the fence we are building or a light switch plate for the tool shed. Indeed, we might not even go buy bricks for the tool shed, but instead might print them from impurities pulled from the air and the dirt beneath our feet. Such a process would both capture carbon in the air to make the bricks and avoid all the carbon involved in making and then transporting traditional bricks to your house.

If it all sounds a little too science fiction, think again. Lowe's has already been honored as a Champion of Change by the US government for its prototype system to recycle plastic (e.g., plastic bags and bottles).[11] The future may be closer than you have imagined. But to get there, Lowe's didn't work alone. It had to work with uncommon partners to create the future.

Uncommon partners are the types of organizations you might not normally work with, but which can greatly help you create radical new futures. Increasingly, as new technologies emerge and old industries converge, companies are finding that working independently to create all the necessary capabilities to enter new industries or create new technologies is costly, risky, and even counterproductive. Instead, organizations are finding that they need to collaborate with uncommon partners as an ecosystem to cocreate the future together. Nathan and his colleague at INSEAD, Andrew Shipilov, call this arrangement an *adaptive ecosystem strategy* and described how companies such as Lowe's, Samsung, Mastercard, and others are learning to work differently with partners and to work with different kinds of partners to more effectively discover new opportunities.[12] For Lowe's, an adaptive ecosystem strategy working with uncommon partners forms the foundation of capturing new opportunities and transforming the company. Despite its increased agility, Lowe's can't be (and shouldn't become) an independent additive-manufacturing, robotics-using, exosuit-building, AR-promoting, fill-in-the-blank-what's-next-ing company in addition to being a home improvement company. Instead, Lowe's applies an adaptive ecosystem strategy to find the uncommon partners with which it can collaborate in new territory.[13]

To apply the adaptive ecosystem strategy with uncommon partners, start by identifying the technical or operational components required for a particular focus area (e.g., exosuits) and then sort these components into three groups. First, there are the components that are emerging organically without any assistance from the orchestrator—the leader who tries to bring together the adaptive ecosystem. Second, there are the elements that might emerge, with encouragement and support. Third are the elements that won't happen unless you do something about it. In an adaptive ecosystem strategy, you can create regular partnerships for the first two elements—those already emerging or that might emerge—if needed. But you have to create the elements in the final category (those that won't emerge) either with an uncommon partner or by yourself.

For example, when Lowe's wanted to explore the additive-manufacturing space, it began a search for an uncommon partner to provide the missing but needed capabilities. Unfortunately, initial discussions with major 3-D printing companies proved disappointing. The major manufacturers kept trying to sell Lowe's 3-D printers. But the vision our group had created with science fiction was not for vendors to sell Lowe's a printer, but for partners to help the company build a system—something that would allow customers to scan, manipulate, print, and eventually recycle additive-manufacturing objects. Every time we discussed 3-D printing systems with these major companies, they responded that they could do it and then tried to sell printers. When Carin Watson, one of the leading lights at Singularity University, introduced us to Made In Space (a company being incubated in Singularity University's futuristic accelerator), we discovered an uncommon partner that understood what it meant to cocreate a system.

Initially, Made In Space had been focused on simply getting 3-D printing to work in space, where you can't rely on gravity, you can't send up a technician if the machine breaks, and you can't release noxious fumes into cramped spacecraft quarters.[14] But after the four days in the conference room going over the comic for additive manufacturing, Made In Space and Lowe's emerged with a bigger vision. The company helped lay out an artifact trail that included not only the first printer on the International Space Station but also printing system services in Lowe's stores.

Of course, the vision for an additive-manufacturing future didn't end there. It also reshaped Made In Space's trajectory, encouraging the startup, during those four days in a NASA conference room, to design a bolder future. Today, some of its bold projects include the Archinaut, a system that enables satellites to build themselves while in space, a direction that emerged partly from the science fiction narrative we created around additive manufacturing.

In summary, uncommon partners help you succeed by providing you with the capabilities you shouldn't be building yourself, as well as with fresh insights. You also help uncommon partners succeed by creating new opportunities from which they can prosper (see the sidebar "Helping Uncommon Partners Prosper").

Narratives Pivot, Principles Don't

In the background of the first Lowe's robots comic, workers moved about the store wearing exosuits—external robotic skeletons. Although the exosuits were originally just a background detail, many people commented that the exosuits seemed really interesting. Although exosuits hadn't been the focus of the story, we thought it might be worth exploring. So we pivoted on the original narrative by creating a second narrative that described how workers in the future would use exosuits to help them work and keep them safe. At the time, exosuits had started to enter the fringes of the scientific frontier, but most of these were hard robotics—large, heavy, motorized mech-inspired machines that were complex and maybe even a bit scary to wear.

Moreover, our interactions with engineers helped us understand how long it would take to develop reliable components for hard

Helping Uncommon Partners Prosper

Working most effectively with uncommon partners can require a shift from more familiar outsourcing or partnership relationships. When working with uncommon partners, you are trying to cocreate the future, which entails a great deal more uncertainty. Because you can't specify outcomes precisely, agreements are typically less formal than in other types of relationships, and they operate under the provisions of shared vision and trust more than binding agreement clauses. Moreover, your goal isn't to extract all the value from the relationship. Rather, you need to find a way to share the value.

Ideally, your uncommon partners should be transformed for the better by the work you do. For example, Lowe's uncommon partner developing the robotics narrative was a small startup called Fellow Robots. Through their work with Lowe's, Fellow Robots transformed from a small team focused on a narrow application of robotics (which was arguably the wrong problem) to a growing company developing a very different and valuable set of capabilities: putting cutting-edge technology on top of the old legacy systems embedded at the core of most companies. Working with Lowe's allowed Fellow Robots to discover new opportunities, and today Fellow Robots works with retailers around the world, including BevMo! and Yamada. Ultimately, working with uncommon partners should be transformative for both of you, so focus more on creating a bigger pie than on how you are going to slice up a smaller pie.

exosuits. Similarly, discussions with risk departments at different organizations helped us understand the incredible savings thresholds we would have to hit to make up for the massive insurance premium increases due to the risk of putting people inside hard robotics. We began to realize we would need a different approach.

Fortunately, about this time we stumbled on an uncommon partner at Virginia Tech. In a quiet corner of the green campus, some of the world's leading engineers are building DARPA-level robotics, but also something much friendlier—the core components for mechanical exosuits that use bendable forms to capture and return a worker's potential energy.

As a result, we had to change the artifact trail to account for this big shift, and we even tweaked the narrative a bit to describe how soft-robotics lift-assistance exosuits that used carbon fiber rods to capture mechanical energy could give workers superpowers in the future by helping do their jobs and stay safe (figure 5-1). But building on the revised artifact trail, we used the technology they already had on hand to quickly prototype a workable exosuit. We could then begin neuroprototyping with workers to understand how they felt as well as testing ergonomics to ensure that the exosuits could work.[15]

What's important is that although we went through several rounds of iteration on the narrative and the artifact trail, we stuck to our experimental design principles. These principles included identifying the key assumptions and then rapid, reliable tests of the key assumptions to start learning as quickly as possible. Even though the form of the robotics had changed, first from a robot in stores, then to exosuits built from hard robotics, then to exosuits built using flexible rods that capture and return potential energy, the process to test and learn did not. And by the way, workers *love* wearing exosuits at work. Who doesn't want to have superpowers? But again, maybe we didn't really need neuroscience to know that dressing up like a robot feels awesome.

Results First

Telenor is one of the world's largest telecom operators with a top position in multiple countries across Europe and Asia. It has developed a reputation as one of the best operators in the world, but like

FIGURE 5-1

Panels from early version of exosuit comic

Source: www.lowesinnovationlabs.com/narrative.

all telecoms, in the face of digital transformation and new challengers like WhatsApp, Telenor is embracing innovation as a way to create new value. In the early days of its transformation, Andrew Kvålseth, a senior leader in the Telenor Group, had a compelling idea. What if the company could create accelerators in each of the countries where it operates to incubate promising startups, learn from them, and, in the spirit of working with uncommon partners, cocreate new opportunities with the best of them? He spent months building support across the group for the promising initiative and eventually presented it to the group executive management committee to launch the program across thirteen operating units. Unfortunately, although the initiative had immense promise, it was turned down.

Discouraged but not deterred, Kvålseth took a new role in Telenor as chief strategy and innovation officer at one of its largest operations, DTAC, in Thailand. At the local level, off the radar of the larger organization, and with a tiny budget, he decided to try out the accelerator concept anyway. Although he started small, in just a few years, the DTAC accelerator was already accumulating compelling results—new ideas, opportunities, and, most importantly, talent that could be recruited to speed DTAC's own transformation. News slowly began to spread inside Telenor about the DTAC accelerator, and soon other companies within the Telenor Group reached out to Kvålseth to learn how to create an accelerator of their own. In the end, and in an ironic twist, he was eventually invited to present at the annual January meeting of top executives and explain how Telenor could adopt the program across the group, as part of its larger transformation into an innovative technology company. Although in the end Kvålseth basically achieved his original objective, he ultimately learned a critical lesson about how to achieve those objectives: results first, not vision first.

Intuitively people inside corporations often want to start by selling a grand vision, raising a huge budget, and then executing on their vision. Sometimes this can work, but it can also be a very dangerous path. It often raises expectations for returns so high that only a perfect storm can yield such returns. It also puts the project under the microscope, to make sure it succeeds, leaving little room for change. Therefore, instead of a vision-first approach, we believe in a results-first approach. Start small, keep it quiet, and accumulate small wins first.

This approach is such a basic principle of transformation that we gave it its own section. Results first is also a fundamental principle of innovation. In this vein, Nathan titled his first book *Nail It Then*

Scale It—to emphasize that although it may feel slow to take the time to get things right (nailing it) compared with starting big (scaling it), changing something after you have scaled it is much slower and will most likely end in failure. Your chances of a successful transformation will be orders of magnitude higher if you can first show results and then convince people to get on board because of those results, not just because of a vision. This is why we have emphasized using experimental design to generate believable fKPIs early on. It is also why we encourage you to think of the small-*t* transformations that can lead to a big-*T* transformation.

The Three Noes

As you accumulate results, you can start to share them more broadly with the organization as part of the transformation journey. But as soon as you do share results, and probably even before you do, you will have to wrestle with the three noes: no to mature metrics, no to money, and no to mature systems.

No to Mature Metrics

There is both ample empirical evidence and intuitive rationale that trying to measure an immature project the way you measure a mature project works poorly. Doing so is like trying to judge the value of a new apple seedling using the same metrics you would use for a mature tree, for example, by counting the number of apples a young seedling produces in the current season. These metrics simply don't make sense. Using such metrics, like return on investment or sales, almost inevitably sets a project up for disappointment and failure. This does not mean that new projects lack rigor or metrics. Rather, they simply have different metrics (see "Digital Toolbox: Metrics for New Projects"). Appropriate metrics can include the depth of the customer problem and the solution's capability to deal with it, or cohort metrics like Google's HEART (happiness, engagement, adoption, retention, and task success) framework or Cisco's "value at risk."[16] For specific projects, because we use applied neuroscience, we prefer to measure the results of quantifiable hypotheses using KPIs tied to neural indicators (see the sidebar "What Is Applied Neuroscience Exactly?" in chapter 4).

No to More Money

As soon as you start to show results, inevitably the corporate obsession with scaling will kick in and you may suddenly find people saying things like "Should we pour some gas on this?" or "Should we scale this up?" There will come a time to scale, but early on, refuse the money and the offers to scale. Your projects need time to be tested and to mature. In explaining this tempered approach to senior executives, we have sometimes even referred to John Steinbeck's novella *Of Mice and Men*. We explain that our projects are the fragile rabbits in the story and that the corporation is Lenny—the big, strong, well-intentioned individual who is going to inadvertently kill the rabbits with his strength. There does come a time when you will scale up (after you have truly validated the key assumptions), but until then, don't allow the excitement to supersede the rigorous testing and maturation process. No one will care when it fails. Say no to the money until the time is right.

No to Mature Systems

Big companies have developed various systems—such as vendor management systems, procurement processes, and promissory services agreements—to manage major projects. Using these systems will slow you down and possibly kill your efforts. You need to find a way around these, particularly anything that is transactional, slow, or combative (involving lots of lawyers or negotiation). For example, most companies have a lengthy master promissory services agreement that will kill off any smaller uncommon partners. Just the legal fees to go through that contract can be more than the annual income of some of the startups. If not the legal fees, then the insurance requirements will bankrupt the smaller uncommon partners you want to work with. Instead of applying mature systems designed for mature projects to immature projects, work with your legal department to find an approach suited for transformation projects. For example, when Cisco's innovation teams wanted to start working with uncommon partners, the legal team put together a short, flexible agreement, in plain English, and these simplified agreements sped up the process significantly.[17] Likewise, Intuit put together a legal framework for internal entrepreneurs, paving the way for experimentation without having to seek permission from the legal office.[18]

To scale your innovation, you will eventually need to plug back into your legacy systems. Nevertheless, at the beginning, don't waste precious energy figuring out how to do that before you have demonstrated success. At the same time, don't make choices that preclude returning to your mature systems in the future.

DIGITAL TOOLBOX

Metrics for New Projects

The topic of how to measure new projects, particularly innovation projects, is starting to receive some much-overdue attention. But finding the latest insights on how to account for innovation and transformation can be time-consuming. On leadingtransformationbook.com we share some materials on the latest thinking on metrics for new projects.

Yea-Sayers

It might seem counterintuitive to talk about yea-saying after a discussion of the three noes, but although we have introduced new tools for transformation, actually leading transformation will be hard. There will be obstacles, resisters, and detractors. The well-established advice about how to spread new things across an organization typically suggests focusing first on the enthusiastic early adopters—people who will be quick to adopt—and high-energy advocates. The next step, convincing the rest of the organization, requires greater effort. The bulk of the organization will fall in line slowly. But for the detractors and late adopters, invest just enough energy so that they don't derail the transformation; otherwise, expect them to get on board late or not at all.[19]

Besides this well-established advice, if you believe in your cause, persist, but do it as a yea-sayer. Generations of thinkers point out that fulfillment comes from doing hard things and that great things are rarely separated from the discouragement and obstacles that almost always accompany them. In reflecting on such challenges, Friedrich Nietzsche, one of the most influential modern philosophers, writes, "Examine the lives of the best and most fruitful people and peoples and ask yourselves whether a tree that is supposed to grow to a proud height can dispense with bad weather and storms; whether misfortune and external resistance, some kinds of hatred, jealousy, stubbornness, mistrust, hardness, avarice, and violence do not belong among the favorable conditions without which any great growth even of virtue is scarcely possible."[20] Alain de Botton, a contemporary philosopher, explains Nietzsche's argument: "Nietzsche was striving to correct the belief that fulfillment must come easily or not at all, a belief ruinous in its effects, for it leads us to withdraw prematurely from challenges that might have been overcome if only we had been prepared for the savagery legitimately demanded by almost everything valuable."[21]

But how should we meet these obstacles? Nietzsche offers advice on how to do just such a thing. In one of his essays, he makes a resolution to be a "yea-sayer," someone who welcomes obstacles rather than resists them: "I want more and more to perceive the necessary characters in things as the beautiful:—I shall thus be one of those who beautify things. Amor fati: let that henceforth be my love! I do not want to wage war with the ugly. I do not want to accuse, I do not want even to accuse the accusers. Looking aside, let that be my sole negation! And all in all, to sum up: I wish to be at any time hereafter only a yea-sayer!"[22]

As you meet resistance, in a counterintuitive approach (or at least counter to what comes naturally) perhaps try first to say yes, rather than no or fighting back. Agreeing can disarm your opponents and may lead to an important insight about how to do things differently. For example, Kyle and Amanda Manna were recently working with an organization (whose identity has been disguised as a part of a nondisclosure agreement) to create a new strategic narrative. They had conducted a number of in-depth interviews to uncover the organizational nomenclature (as described in chapter 3) and found that the organization saw itself as a creator of art. After going through the science fiction and strategic narrative process, which produced a compelling future vision, Kyle and Manna were in the middle of working with external graphic artists to design the comic when they got a call from a senior executive at the client who demanded that their team would need to be involved in any artistic endeavor for it to be adopted.

This is where the instinct to be a perennial yea-sayer kicks in. Of course, in an organization that is differentiated by its artistic style, they should have anticipated skepticism about outside parties creating art for the organization. This was actually one of the best things that could have happened. If the strategic narrative came from within, there was a much greater chance of successfully changing behaviors and attitudes in the organization. So they responded by saying, "Yes, of course, we would love for you to help create the graphic novel." Kyle and Amanda's yea-sayer attitude saved the project. Of course, being a yea-sayer can't solve everything, and we aren't suggesting that you should be obsequious and thereby lead a transformation so burdened by internal demands that it becomes unwieldy (which is why we encouraged you earlier to keep things quiet until you have more progress). But we are proposing that you approach any resistance, negativity, and discouragement with a yes. Be a yea-sayer.

Transformation from Ossified to Agile

In this book, we have talked about a process to dream bigger and transform organizations. We used the transformation at Lowe's as a red thread throughout the book to illustrate how a prototypical organization—mature, profitable, and focused on operational excellence—can transform. We described some incredible innovation leaps made along the way. But the innovations themselves were just a Trojan horse for the larger goal of transforming the organization. For this reason, we told stories of other companies with which we have worked (those that we can reveal), like Svensk Film and IKEA, and how they transformed themselves when it was less about technology and more about strategy, business models, or culture. Ultimately, whether or not a transformation involves technology, and whether or not you start with little-*t* transformations as we recommended, creating a strategic narrative, thoughtfully breaking bottlenecks, and creating fKPIs to guide your future will help you overcome the people problems that impede every transformation.

Lowe's succeeded in building its way through the valley of deceptive disappointment to create differentiating technologies and solutions. But more impressive has been the start of a transformation inside Lowe's. Today, narrative has become a focal point of almost every activity. Leaders inside the company also see their roles in a new, more empowered, more proactive light. By applying the transformation process described in this book, the company has started to shift from the prototypical big company to a very different organization, one that sees what could be.

In the future, users could engage with Lowe's products from anywhere in the world, independently of physical locations. Or Lowe's could become much more than just a mere pipeline for others' products and instead could become a materials company or an IP company, or whatever fulfills the purpose of helping people love where they live. Of course, the company still has bureaucracy, politics, and everything else—all organizations are still populated by human beings with all our associated weaknesses. But Lowe's has a different feeling than it once had.

The beginning of the transformation journey at Lowe's gives hope that other organizations can do so as well. Whether Lowe's continues on its transformation journey depends on applying the process described in this book to keep reengineering its future. Fortunately, we have seen other rigid organizations and even their most rigid organizational functions become the most agile. Risk and legal groups became our advocates. Executives who had previously viewed innovation with skepticism became capable practitioners of it. It is possible to become a nimble competitor ready for a new world. What must change is the belief that the organization can do it. In leading transformation, you need to believe that people want to do big things. Believe that they will adapt. And then take charge of your future. There is no objective future; there is only the future that you create.

The Behavioral Innovation Manifesto

New Approaches for a World of Uncertainty

In 1850, the president of Harvard University remarked in surprise that over half of its graduates were going into a new profession, one that hadn't even existed a few decades earlier.[1] Although people were flocking to this new profession, no schools yet trained those wanting to join its ranks, and no programs existed to provide certifications. Yet this new profession would go on to become the largest professional class in history, spawning thousands of new colleges, programs, and schools.

This new profession, which today we call management, hadn't previously existed because there had been no need for it before the industrial revolution. At that time, pre–industrial revolution, virtually all companies were small businesses, with thirty or fewer people employed in small workshops. But during the industrial revolution, the social order that had existed for centuries began to rapidly change. First, the formation of the Dutch East India Company in the 1600s laid the groundwork for the large corporation, with the creation of joint stock ownership. Then, technology, particularly the steam engine, changed the entire economic landscape, transforming it from an ecosystem of small workshops into a handful of giant organizations. Suddenly, the world faced new problems, namely, how to coordinate the exploding rail system so the trains ran on time, how to hire the armies of laborers now needed and how to pay them for their work, how to optimize production, and how to coordinate a huge enterprise. Business schools were founded to train the leaders who could solve these problems, primarily how to coordinate, optimize, and compete. Frederick Winslow Taylor, the father of modern management, was literally trying to answer the question of what size of shovel to use when a worker was shoveling iron ore, and at what pace, to optimize production. At the heart of these challenges was the question of how to capture value in the gold rush created by industrial manufacturing technology.

But in the last few decades, new forms of digital technology, starting with the transistor and all its digital ancestors, including microprocessors, sensors, and connectivity, have again transformed that landscape. Digital technologies have lowered the barriers to participate and create while magnifying the potential impact of such participation. So have geopolitical, social, and educational changes. As more and more individuals participate, the pace of invention, creation, and adoption has exploded while the dominance of big companies has fallen. For example, consider that the US patent application rate increased more than sevenfold.[2] Over fifty million new businesses are created each year worldwide today.[3] Meanwhile, from the 1930s until today, the number of years a *Fortune* 500 company stays on that list of titans has fallen from seventy-five to just eleven.[4]

In this more uncertain environment, the problems we face are less and less about how to capture value, which was the primary concern during the first industrial revolution, and more and more about how to iterate, explore, and innovate or, more generally, how to create value. But if the primary occupation of classical management has been capturing value in a world of relative certainty, what are the right frameworks for creating value in a world of uncertainty?

Classical management has comparatively little of substance to say on this front. As the environment continues to become more uncertain and complex, leaders will require new perspectives and tools to solve new problems.

Fortunately, many new frameworks have emerged to fill this need. In computer science, agile methodologies emphasizing rapid sprints and iterative cycles were developed as a reaction to the failure of earlier waterfall planning methodologies (sequential approaches in which one step is not initiated until the preceding step is completed). Similarly, human-centered design that expresses empathy for customer problems was a reaction to more-traditional stage-gate product development. Likewise, the lean-startup methodology, focusing on rapid experimentation and minimum viable products, was created to countervail the armchair-quarterback approaches to business planning. Similarly, business model innovation approaches have become popular and highlight the possibilities of creating value with new business models.

Each of these frameworks has added immensely to our emerging understanding of how to manage in a world of uncertainty. But are they the complete answers? Does the lean startup offer all that we need in this complex world? Possibly not. Although each framework offers useful tools, they may offer only part of the eventual solution set for a world of uncertainty.[5] Indeed, as a thought experiment, ask yourself, Is design thinking or the lean-startup approach likely to produce the next SpaceX, the next AI breakthrough, or the next figurative transistor? Or does making a "moonshot" require something different—imagination, commitment, and even denial of easily observed consumer reactions (consumers hated the Aeron chair, and Steve Jobs notoriously refused to listen to customer feedback on radical products). Just as it took almost two hundred years from the start of the industrial revolution to the formation of the first business school (in 1881) and then another century to refine the discipline of management, it may take more time to develop the mature discipline to navigate uncertainty and value creation.

Arguably, more radical innovations are characterized by both more uncertainty and situations with greater experimentation costs (the costs of experimenting with reusable rockets are orders of magnitude greater than those associated with app development) (see figure 2-1).[6] As Nathan argues in his previous book, we should be looking more broadly for the theories and frameworks that are still missing, the theories that would help us better navigate and prosper from both uncertainty and opportunity.[7]

This book represents one of these frameworks, particularly in its attention to the behavioral limitations that keep us from seeing and capturing radical opportunities or transformational changes. But it does not represent the full spectrum of ideas, frameworks, or theories that can help us prosper in an uncertain world.

The Behavioral Innovation Opportunity

There are more opportunities, theories, and frameworks than just those described in this book. We face an opportunity for a behavioral revolution in innovation and transformation by understanding and addressing the human roadblocks to transformational change. Just as economics has been transformed by a behavioral perspective showing how cognitive factors (i.e., the human elements) reshape our understanding of rational decision making, so can a behavioral revolution in innovation and transformation revolutionize how we see these disciplines, primarily by uncovering and addressing the human limits to these activities. Since we have focused on the behavioral limits to transformation in this book, let us focus a moment on innovation (although the same observations apply to transformation).

Behavioral innovation can be defined as the application of cognitive sciences (e.g., psychology, applied neuroscience) to study the microprocesses of innovation (including the biases that limit innovation) and the mechanisms to address these biases. Thus, behavioral innovation is as much a scaffolding for a conversation between disciplines as it is a new discipline to examine how innovation and transformation happen. In suggesting such a behavioral revolution, we are not ignoring other people's efforts to study the role of psychology, emotion, perception, and other forces on innovation. Clearly, many others have made valiant efforts. But the business world lacks a more systematic view of the problems or their proposed solutions— a view like that emerging in behavioral economics. A study of such problems and solutions may now be particularly promising, since the emerging application of neuroscience to innovation might take us a step beyond prior behavioral revolutions. Rather than just identifying that there are biases, as behavioral economics has done, neuroscience can define precisely where and when biases occur and then develop prescriptive tools to address these biases.

For example, the behavioral transformation process described in this book represents our attempt to contribute to this conversation by integrating psychological and neurological perspectives to help people overcome many common barriers to innovation and transformation. But the process we describe is simply one small component of the larger conversation; it neither describes the entire domain of behavioral innovation nor contains all the answers that may emerge from this new domain. By contrast, as a discipline, behavioral innovation, or behavioral transformation, can reshape how we think about innovation, change, and reaching our potential both as individuals and as organizations. Below we briefly describe some inspiration for the opportunities in such a conversation.

Behavioral Innovation Draws on Multiple Fields

As a domain, behavioral innovation draws on multiple fields, particularly the cognitive sciences, to understand the forces shaping innovation microprocesses and how to transform them. For example, although psychology has been seriously applied to economic decision making, far fewer have studied how psychology affects innovation. For example, psychological studies have shown that people tend toward incremental innovation. By contrast, we praise innovators who, like Elon Musk, seem to break free of incrementalism to revolutionize new domains like space travel, transportation, and energy. But we have paid far less attention to how people like Musk make long, imaginative leaps than we have to the importance of such leaps. Likewise, narrative and emotion are rarely discussed as serious elements of innovation, beyond their ability to persuade investors. But narratives are one of the oldest, most intuitive tools; they are wired deep in the brain, and their full potential remains to be understood and applied.

Similarly, our emotions aren't entirely separate from our decision making. Yet the conversation about the emotional side of decision making rarely gets serious attention beyond crude descriptors like intuition or gut feel (for a notable exception, see the work of professor Quy Huy).[8] Finally, beyond the kinds of neural indicators discussed here, neuroscience holds immense potential to reveal, through big data, the precise source of the biases that impede us and to suggest how to counteract them. Indeed, applied neuroscience might ultimately reshape human behavior and beliefs. In sum, these cognitively related fields—psychology, neuroscience, semiotics, and other fields—promise to help us more deeply understand and overcome the forces that hold us back from more-desirable futures.

Behavioral Innovation Provides Insights on Innovation Processes

These interdisciplinary lenses can provide insight on how to create real innovation and transformation. For example, the search for, commitment to, and development of innovations—at the heart of our story here—can be viewed in a new light, through a behavioral innovation lens. Rather than just asking people to innovate, which seems to be the current demand in most big organizations, if we could understand the psychological, cognitive, and identity biases that stymie innovation, we could better confront them.[9] For example, studies Thomas conducted with his students reveal that simply explaining the elements of creativity to people can increase their creativity by 30 percent on average (range, 15 to 200 percent).[10] We are currently studying how our natural predilections for being early adopters, for art or science, for certain careers, or for personality traits affects how we look for and respond to new ideas. In the future, we could match these predilections to gene types to understand the interplay between biology and choice in creativity. Alternatively, we could uncover the antecedents and obstacles to negative capability, or the ability to entertain uncertainty. Perhaps most importantly, we could design more tools like those described in this book to overcome the behavioral tendencies in the search for innovation or the execution of transformation. For example, we have described using science fiction as a tool to overcome the psychological tendency to search locally for new ideas, but what other tools could we use to imagine the adjacent possible?

Likewise, although some good research has been done on how the commitment to pursue uncertain innovations emerges and evolves (e.g., the critical role of interpretation and framing), there is still an incredible amount to understand.[11] For example, what aspects of the structure, content, and channel of a narrative produce commitment? Why, for example, did comic books yield so much more commitment among readers than other approaches did? If everyone starts using comics, will the mere exposure dull their impact, or is the blend of visual and textual motivating in an enduring way? What is the role of reason versus emotion in commitment, and which comes first, or how are they intertwined? What impact do nonnarrative tools have on the suspension of disbelief and in creating commitment (e.g., tangible artifacts, analogies, metaphors)? How do we move beyond simplified tools, like archetypes, to understand the scales of behavioral tendencies that affect how people commit themselves or change their commitments? What are the biases and other limitations of our existing approaches? For example, what are the motivational alternatives to the "burning platform" approach that so many companies try to use for transformation (named after the now famous email from Nokia's CEO trying to motivate a company transformation in response to the smartphone era set off by Apple, by describing their company as standing on a "burning platform.") Do many our existing frameworks reinforce or counteract the tendency towards incrementalism (e.g., the tendency of the lean-startup approach or design thinking to reinforce local searching)?

Finally, in the development of innovation, neuroscience shows incredible promise to shape the direction, adaptation, and governance of innovation. For example, several once-radical innovations are now quite ordinary to us (consider that at the start of the twentieth century, flying in an airplane was the realm of fantasy and that, by the end of that century, most people only concerned themselves with complaining about a late flight departure). In studying neurological responses to new things, how do we accurately parse out which innovations consumers might adopt in the future, and which things are just too novel? And how will the responses evolve over time as the innovations become more familiar? Alternatively, how do different types of framing affect our commitment to, our development of, or our acceptance of an innovation (e.g., framing in terms of outcomes, aspirations, or analogies)? Despite some good work in both neuroscience and creativity, many questions remain unanswered.[12] These questions represent important opportunities to understand innovation, transformation, and change through a more integrative behavioral lens.

Moving Forward

In this book, we have raised more questions than we answered. We have tried to suggest that behavioral innovation and transformation could be new disciplines for a world of increasing uncertainty. These disciplines have relevance to both practitioners and academics and to organizations and individuals. We don't claim to have all the answers, but we are simply extending an invitation to join us in the search for them. If all of us are going to create the futures we desire, we need new tools, new approaches, and new inspiration. We are working toward creating the Transformation Lab, which could be a place to explore these ideas. Together, as uncommon partners, we can create that world—the world we want to live in together.

Leading Transformation in Your Own Life

Could the ideas from behavioral transformation be applied to transform an individual life? Consider one poignant case study.

Seeing Possibilities That Lie in Plain Sight

David Whyte, a best-selling author, describes the moment when he realized he could change from an unfulfilling career in marine biology to his current vocation. Originally he had been attracted to marine biology while watching Jacques Cousteau films as a boy. But after many years of university study, he found himself working long hours at a desk writing repetitive educational modules, far from the ocean. For a time, the work had been satisfying because of the greater educational purpose. But slowly, the repetition and distance from the adventure of the ocean began to grind him down.

One day, a man asked him to lunch, explaining that he wanted to get to know Whyte and ask his advice about a tidal floodgate. Whyte describes his frustration that the man assumed he could so casually interrupt Whyte's work to ask for free advice. But he also felt curiosity, which led him to accept the invitation. When they did eventually sit down to lunch, the man described how a tidal gate, installed several decades earlier in the sound, had interrupted the salmon migration pattern that was tens of thousands of years old. The man asked if Whyte had any ideas what they could do about it. Whyte had no answers but promised to think about it.

But that night, as Whyte reflected, he found himself thinking about the salmon, trapped in the tidal inlet, held back from a migration pattern they had known from centuries. Suddenly, reflecting on this image, he found himself doing something unusual. He started to write a poem. The poem opened with these lines:

> *For too many days now I have not written of the sea,*
> *nor the rivers, nor the shifting currents*
> *we find between the islands.*[1]

In the poem, Whyte asks himself why he isn't paying attention to the deeper currents in his own life, the currents of what he really wants to do in his life.

Today, looking back on this poem, Whyte describes it as a pivotal moment, when he realized he needed to shift from his career in marine biology. The poem (which is in itself a form of story), and the reflection, gave him permission to ask a more powerful question about another possible future—an adjacent possibility—that he found more inspiring. It also gave him the roughest of maps about what to do about it. Today, Whyte is one of the best-known modern poets. He works not just with readers and writers, but also regularly with corporations to help them see their work in a new way.

By the way, Whyte did help restore the natural tidal opening to the stream, and the salmon returned to their ancient migratory path after decades of absence. He also helped create community awareness about the impact on the salmon and worked with local farmers to shift their practices to lessen their negative impact on the salmon. Today the salmon are an integral part of the local community. And the poem that Whyte composed back then ends with these lines:

> *But now I have spoken of that great sea,*
> *The ocean of longing shifts through me*
> *The blessed inner star of navigation*
> *Moves in the dark sky above*
> *And I am ready like the young salmon*
> *To leave his river, blessed with hunger,*
> *For a great journey on the drawing tide.*[2]

In many ways, his poem reflects what we have been trying to say all along about strategic narrative for organizations.

Which Possibilities Aren't We Seeing?

If science fiction can help large organizations see new possibilities and a poem could help Whyte find an alternate career, why can't the tools we described help individuals see new possibilities and take action? The behavioral challenges at the individual level are very similar to those at the organizational level. Incremental search, habit, and fear hold back individuals just as much as they hold back organizations. Behavioral transformation tools can help us see new possibilities we aren't now seeing; the tools can give us the courage to break free of our habits to do something meaningful about it.

We have begun to experiment with a process to effect a behavioral transformation at the individual level. We borrow some of the same tools simply because they are strong counteragents to the behavioral biases we identified. At the individual level, you start the process by using narratives to imagine a different future. As an individual, it may be difficult to access science fiction writers to imagine a new story about yourself (and you would need to provide them a good deal of source material). So instead, consider starting to gather inspirational stories from different sources: those written by yourself and those written by others.

For the latter, we recommend reaching out to several people whom know you well (the more the better) and ask them, "Using what you know about me (who I am, what makes me happy, what I am good at), could you write two or three short stories (one or two paragraphs) about what my life could look like in five years?" Ask them to write about the adjacent possible, that is, alternative futures that they imagine could make you happy. Tell them, "The goal is to stretch the imagination and really visualize what could be possible. So if two of your stories could really push the boundaries of what might make me happy, I would appreciate it." Give people a short time frame (one or two weeks). If you have a significant other, ask for at least two or three stories.

Then sit down by yourself and work on writing stories about what your life could look like. Try to create a visual setting that describes what you do, how you do it, where you do it, and when you do it. The goal of the stories is to explore different possibilities, not to be all-inclusive. You aren't trying to write a single story in which you live on a yacht and a publisher helicopters in to give you book offers, or whatever your dream is. Instead, you are trying to explore, in detail, single specific alternative futures. For example, when we do this exercise for ourselves, we create different life scenarios, such as life as a university professor, a pathbreaking neuroscientist, an independent author, a CEO, and a social-change agent. We also play with the forms. Nathan prefers short paragraphs or bullet points. Kyle prefers to write next year's Christmas card, but he writes it in January and imagines what could have happened by the end of the year.

To get started on your own stories, you might try a series of prompts. For example, in your different stories, ask yourself questions like these: What would be my ideal future in five years (future view)? What would be an ideal daily-life work pattern (daily-life view)? What would be my ideal relationship (relationship view)? What outcomes would I like to have achieved in five years (outcomes view)? What would be the worst-case scenario for my life in five years (opposite view)?

If these prompts feel too generic, then try asking yourself more-specific questions, like these: Where do I live, and where could I live part-time? What do I want to learn? What hobbies do I have? If I could choose any job or craft, what would it be? What do I want my evenings to look like? Mornings? If I could make up a new daily routine, what would it be? How could I create a nonroutine? What would the most alive version of me do? The most playful version? What would I never do if I could avoid it?

In writing these stories, recall that it is easy to see your current work as the enemy and that the grass is always greener on the other side. Not everyone needs to move out of a career in marine biology and go into poetry. Most of us will probably stay in our current careers, partly to earn a living or support those we love, but we could stay in our careers a different way. For this reason, many of your questions should ask about seeing or doing your work in a different way or doing different work where you are. To see these things differently, you may find it helpful to identity a handful of heroes and explore how they work. What traits do you admire about how they live or think? Integrate these ideas into your narrative of how you work.

Accumulate these stories, both your own and those from friends who know you well, and pay attention to what resonates with you. Hopefully there are lots of offbeat details and complete fantasies. This is a good thing. You are trying to push the boundaries of your thinking beyond the everyday routine that you are executing. Then try to synthesize these stories into a single master narrative. The synthesis can be difficult; you can leave a few loose threads in the story. But over a modest period, try to answer for yourself which story describes the future you want to create in five years. Then write a story that describes this vision, your inner star. You will return to this story in the future, and you may revise it. But ultimately, the story should help you both see, and believe in, what is possible.

As you consolidate and synthesize your story, next lay out the artifact trail to get there. Draw on the steps we described earlier in the book. The trail should have specific, achievable small wins that you could accomplish in a week or a few weeks, followed by other, more aggressive, but measurable and achievable objectives, leading up to your eventual end goal.

So, for example, if you, like David Whyte, wanted to become an author, your artifact trail should not simply be to quit your job tomorrow (unless you have serious financial freedom to do so). It should contain the small action steps to get there. For example, every Saturday morning, you are going to commit to write for two hours the first thing in the morning. Two days a week, you will go into work a bit late or wake up a little earlier to write. Each month, in the evenings, you will read one book that either represents beautiful writing or talks about writing. These would be your early artifacts. Artifacts can be events or outcomes (e.g., I registered for a course), or they can be microhabits just as we described (e.g., on Saturday morning, I'm going to get up early and write). Later artifacts on your artifact trail would be to share your writing with others, to submit your writing to be published, and so forth. But whatever the specific content of your artifact trail, as we discussed earlier, it needs to be specific enough to allow you to overcome the key behavioral limitations—the routines that keep you doing the same thing every day.

Be sure to apply the right tools to counteract the fear of uncertainty. When leading a transformation, we proposed using experimental design and applied neuroscience as data-based indicators of the best direction for an innovation. These indicators provide positive feedback and signposts when you are pioneering new territory; they help you overcome the fear that often leads to retreat or retrenchment. The question then becomes what tools at the individual level you can use to counteract the fear that you will encounter.

It would be hard to use applied neuroscience to measure your own brain reactions. Instead, you may want to start by very clearly stating your premises (or reasons for making a transformative change), the obstacles that will create fear, and your plan for addressing them when the time comes. You might also create a personal real-options strategy (*real options* is a term borrowed from finance and strategy where you create multiple options to explore the future). For example, when we interviewed Ben Feringa, a Nobel Prize winner in chemistry, he shared a piece of wisdom we've heard echoed by many others who navigate uncertainty to do great things. Feringa tells his students, "You always want two feet to stand on—a safe project and a risky project. That way, if the risky project fails, you have a safe project to go back to. And if you don't have a safe project, you will chase a failing risky project way too far down the road before calling it quits."[3] What are your own personal real options?

Finally, you may simply need to let go of the mindset that life is about eliminating risks and optimizing outcomes—a worldview that comes too easily to many of us—and recognize that uncertainty comes as a by-product of pursuing new possibilities. Discomfort with the uncertainty is normal, but try to play with the possibilities rather than control them. In other words, apply a bit of negative capability to see what the future may bring.

Our Origin Stories

The sparks of *Leading Transformation* were ignited in various places: in the jungles of Costa Rica, during the frozen nights of an isolated Norwegian town north of the Arctic Circle, and inside the sheltering Eucalyptus groves of Stanford campus. Despite these dramatically different starting points by three collaborators, we all sought to answer the same question—how do we create breakthrough change? (We use the term *change* broadly to apply to a transformational innovation, initiative, strategy, or another change.) And we all converged on the same answer. In our separate quests, we discovered a process that works to envision and capture breakthrough opportunities, meaning we have applied it to transform real organizations, not just the Googles of the world, but also the average, everyday companies. Although nothing is perfect, we believe that the process can help you transform your organization, and even your life, by providing you with the tools to envision and then create your best possible future. Given that we talk about some unconventional new ideas for transformation, such as using science fiction, comic books, and applied neuroscience, we thought that it would be more fun to talk about ourselves using comic books to tell our own origin stories (see Appendix C).

Kyle Nel: How Do We Change Calcified Organizations?

While pursuing his MBA, with a focus on behavioral marketing and management, Kyle first saw and realized that what people say often don't match up to their actions, not because they lied but because stated intent is just not a great predictor of behavior. After this experience, Kyle firmly believed that people are all much more "predictably irrational" than they would like to admit. He started to notice that transformation occurred when people worked together that normally would not, becoming uncommon partners.

In order to prove this theory, Kyle finished his MBA program and joined the biggest organization of them all—Walmart. He started looking for behavioral data that could unlock the mystery of why people do the things that they do. And by looking at data such as what consumers searched for online, what they bought—and what they never bought more than once—he was able to uncover the power of behavioral data to provide more accurate guidance. He was able to show the potentially significant impact of relatively small levers to start changing the organization. But it wasn't financial impact that led new tools to be adopted within Walmart, but the story. If one manager heard a colleague's a story about how a tool saved the day, the manager's immediate response was, "How do I get it?" And once they obtained the tool, then they started using it. Kyle could see that it was more than just the power of data that persuaded; it was also the power of story that was changing the company.

As Kyle put his ideas about human behavior into practice, he was succeeding at creating smaller transformations that could add up to real change. He saw an opportunity to test out his ideas at even greater scale. While at Walmart he was recruited to join Lowe's, the home improvement retailer, with a vision of how to change behavior inside and outside of the organization. And eventually, he got his chance—working with science fiction writers to explore probable, possible futures and turning those stories into an innovation strategy, delivered via comic books.

The process itself was still rudimentary, consisting of three primary elements: (1) visionary storytelling through science fiction to create meaningful narratives about possible futures, (2) a tangible artifact trail to create and maintain momentum with small wins, and (3) meaningful data to guide the development journey using neuroprototyping. Later the process would become more sophisticated and take into account, for example, the decision politics and bottlenecks of an organization, and many other tools.

But from that core framework, the process was applied over and over to help Lowe's begin a transformation, moving from a calcified, risk-averse, hierarchical organization into an adaptive organization capable of moving quickly on new opportunities rather than debating endlessly. The conventional retailer moved to the forefront of technologies like AR, additive manufacturing, robotics, and exosuits. The developments at Lowe's caused others to reach out—companies like Google, Microsoft, and IKEA, as well as academic, nonprofit, and governmental organizations—asking how they could replicate the process. By then, Kyle's path had already intersected with those of Thomas and Nathan, and the three began constructing the full, more robust process behind leading transformation.

Thomas Zoëga Ramsøy: Why Do We Do What We Do?

Looking out the café window, Thomas could see a pod of killer whales break through the icy water, barely visible in the dim light of midday Tromsø, a small Norwegian island north of the Arctic Circle. In the distance, the mountains rose like cruel teeth, and above them, the indescribable stage of sky would play host to the northern lights in a few hours. In a strange way, this isolated town at the reach of civilization seemed the perfect place to study that most introspective of subjects—the human mind. In this icy wasteland, stomping through snow so cold it squeaked, Thomas puzzled over what would become a lifelong obsession: how does the mind shape why we do what we do?

Although most of us believe we are rational and infallible, much of the time our thinking is incredibly biased. One extreme example Thomas studied illustrates the extent to which we can be blind to our own bias. Having fallen from a ladder and injured his head, the man, in his forties, seemed perfectly normal on a first encounter. But there was a slight disconnect that was the wedge into something more. He and Thomas could discuss art, philosophy, and everyday life, but he often seemed to be reflecting back what Thomas had already said. Soon Thomas noticed that he would actually mimic Thomas's every gesture, like a mirror. More worrying, on closer examination, the man was neither capable of initiating planned behaviors or inhibiting impulses. He could explain, in detail, how he would leave Thomas's office after the session, walk up the corridor to the kiosk, and buy some cigarettes. But he would never actually get up and do it on his own; he would sit there until prompted. He also became hypersexual (toward his wife, who could not even recognize him anymore), hyperoral (cigarettes, candy, etc.), and dysexecutive (among other symptoms, losing any impulse control).

Worst of all, he had lost the ability to understand his own dysfunctions. He still insisted he was perfectly normal. His injury made him completely lacking in empathy, unable to recognize his wife's tears during joint meetings. The experience imprinted on Thomas just how central the brain is to our unique human nature: our ability to be social, to plan, to adjust our behaviors and choices. And the experience underscored just how biased we can all be, whether we are extremely biased, as in this case, or mildly biased. All of us create a polished narrative that everything is as it is supposed to be—something researchers such as Michael Gazzaniga have coined the *narrator* of the brain.

If our brains and biases are so powerful and challenging to understand directly, Thomas began to wonder, could we use neuroscience to peer into the inner mechanisms of our minds to better explain why we do what we do and potentially how to change it? After earning a PhD in neurobiology, Thomas went on to cofound the Decision Neuroscience Research Group, formed jointly between Copenhagen Business School and Copenhagen University Hospital. The group, which later became the Center for Decision Neuroscience, was involved in raising more than half a billion Danish kroner (about US$80 million) to take the step that behavioral economics had failed to take: to study the mechanisms that create that bias and, perhaps, how to develop tools to reshape our actions. For example, some of Thomas's early research led to groundbreaking studies on the incredible neural activity that occurs in the transition from subconscious to conscious thought. The research reveals how frequently we rely on subconscious, but biased, thinking described by Daniel Kahneman in his *Thinking, Fast and Slow*.

It was a meeting of minds, then, when, one snowy January morning, Kyle and Thomas met for the first time outside a Copenhagen restaurant to discuss the possibility of using neuroscience to overcome the biases that hold us back from effective change. After a hasty, excited meal, the duo retreated to Thomas's office to frame up a critical challenge: could they use neuroscience to create indicators of how people respond to innovation and change? At first, Thomas was skeptical. There had been so much bad science, particularly in neuromarketing, that he had launched a blog called *BrainEthics*, attacking the black-box, hand-waving neurobabble being sold to big companies as science. Thomas argued that to tackle the biases that stop transformational change, we didn't need to understand the brain better; much work had already been done to understand the functioning of the brain. Rather, we needed to develop scientifically valid, quantifiable measures of brain activity (measures based on well-developed neuroscience) and then correlate these observations with actual behaviors.

Thomas began pulling textbooks off the shelf, and as he read chapter after chapter, constructing measures, he began to lay the foundations for neuro-indicators that could do what had never been done before—provide data-based predictors of how innovations might be adopted or rejected by consumers. These indicators, based on openly published and scientifically validated standards, would later become the foundations for applied neuroscience and neuro-prototyping—a set of tools that can predict how users respond to innovation and change. As described in the book, these indicators provide signposts in the wilderness of uncertainty that accompanies change, not unlike the wilderness of Tromsø. They show the direction that pathbreaking transformers should take as they pursue innovation and change initiatives.

Nathan Furr: What Are the Theories for a World of Uncertainty?

As Nathan walked down the rocky trough of the deep canyon, dusk began to set in, accentuating the thick rock walls bent like ribbons by an ancient cataclysm that had turned the ancient sea floor upward to meet the sky. Below him, at the mouth of the canyon, the orderly lines of city lights were turning on, yellowed by distance, in the geometric grid of the university, with the business school pinned to the edge of campus. As the sky began to darken, the questions continued to swirl. A young assistant professor, Nathan had been chastised for wasting his time writing books that spoke to management practice. He had been told instead to focus on the academic research that would get him tenure. But as he hiked down the canyon, with the infinity of stars appearing above him, he wondered how he could contain his curiosity at a universe so grand, so full of possibilities. Just as there were so many other stars, how many more questions remained to be asked? How many theories to be discovered?

On the campus below, few remembered that the business school was a recent addition to the edge of campus, just as the management discipline itself was a recent invention. The field of management had been created during the industrial revolution to meet the challenge of coordinating and optimizing the giant corporations created by new technologies. It had taken two centuries between the start of the industrial revolution and the creation of the first MBA program to find the answer, and another century to turn the management discipline into a global machine for training the world's leaders. Now management appeared as a monolithic institution with all the answers.

But the order hid a growing chaos created by another technological revolution. Just as the steam engine had spawned the first industrial revolution, the transistor had created a different kind of revolution, which had been building over the last few decades. In effect, the microprocessor and then the internet had lowered the barriers to participation for generations of entrepreneurs, creating the most uncertain and dynamic landscape in history. Every year, an estimated fifty million new businesses were forming.[1] The rate of invention had increased sixfold since the 1960s.[2] The pace of new technology competition increases every year.[3] The new ideas, businesses, and technologies created—as ever more people engaged with the creation economy—were changing the landscape at an accelerating pace. Indeed, Nathan's own children would face a completely different landscape. According to the World Economic Forum, 65 percent of the jobs they might take when they finish their education don't even exist yet.[4]

As Nathan neared the bottom of the canyon, he wondered, Do we have the theories we need for this new world of uncertainty? Although classical management worked well to coordinate massive organizations for optimizing the production of known products and activities, were these same tools and theories appropriate for creating this new world?

Some alternative theories had started to emerge. During his PhD studies at Stanford, Nathan had been part of the lean-startup movement, writing one of the first books on the movement. Lean startups rejected the business-planning approach to entrepreneurship, inherited from classical management, in favor of a rapid cycle of hypothesis testing more appropriate for conditions of uncertainty. But while at Stanford, Nathan had also witnessed the founding of the design school. Design thinking, itself a reaction to classical product development paradigms in engineering, emphasized human-centered design over product specifications created in the absence of real user needs. Meanwhile, in the computer science department and in the broader Silicon Valley, agile methodologies had emerged as a reaction to waterfall software design. Agile methods emphasized fast sprints and then reflective cycles of learning instead of Gantt charts defining long software-development timelines. These theories had exploded in popularity in the broader business environment, as substitutes for, or complements to, classical management.

But as practitioners of each domain began to argue about which framework was right, Nathan began to wonder, Should we instead be asking which theories are actually missing? If it had taken three centuries to develop classical management in response to the first industrial revolution, how long would it take to develop the new theories for a world of uncertainty? Are we perhaps only just starting to develop the theories for a world of uncertainty?

Indeed, as the sky blackened with the fall of the night, and as Mars appeared as a tiny orange point above the horizon, Nathan wondered, Would lean startup give us the next SpaceX? Would design thinking give us the next transistor? What other theories might we need for a world of uncertainty and might still need to be discovered?

Reaching the bottom of the canyon, Nathan made a resolution: despite the advice to devote himself exclusively to academic publications, which focus on deep validation that often progresses very slowly, he would also devote some of his time to wild ideas, searching for these new theories, even if they later took decades to prove in traditional academic channels. Already, he envisioned a dozen books he would write, even if no one wanted to publish them. Never mind trying to do things only one way! A world of uncertainty is also a world of possibility. He decided to dedicate himself to exploring these new possibilities, new theories, new questions, and new answers, just as much as his dedication to proving them robustly in the academic world.

Fast-forward a few years. As Kyle and Nathan sat across a café table discussing how to use science fiction to break free of the constraints in our own imagination and to envision valuable new futures, it dawned on Nathan that here was a piece of the puzzle. Although the book that he, Kyle, and Thomas were writing would be about how leaders could use science fiction and applied neuroscience to transform organizations, they were all collectively on the trail of something bigger. Recently, the field of economics had been transformed through the application of psychology to reveal how we actually make decisions. The new discipline was called *behavioral economics*. Similarly, the field of innovation and transformation was ripe for change. We could apply psychology to the domain of innovation and transformation to finally uncover the unaddressed biases that derail innovation, and by identifying these biases, we could contend with them. Moreover, rather than create a long list of biases without solutions, we could use applied neuroscience to uncover exactly where the problems occur and design tools to overcome them. This new discipline, *behavioral innovation and transformation*, wouldn't be the one and only answer to how to live in a world of uncertainty, but it could be one of several new theories. Behavioral innovation and transformation could help us overcome our behavioral bottlenecks to see the future. It could help us reach those stars so distant and discover the many opportunities we just don't see yet.

The Hero's Journey: Your Journey

In his classic text, Joseph Campbell describes how our lives follow familiar archetypes, with the hero's journey being at the center. In the hero's journey, an individual sets out on a quest and is helped along the way, at just the right moment, by others who are also on their own quest. Together, they help each other each reach their own particular goals.[5]

This book is the result of our own journeys: the manager who has actually done it, the neuroscientist who could design the tools to overcome our biases, and the academic who could explain why it worked and how to use it. Although we each developed different parts of this book, we see the quest to create breakthrough change as our shared journey. But the book describes not only our journey, but your journey as well, because this book is part of your own quest to create change.

A Summary of the Book Presented as a Graphic Novel

BACK IN 2012, LOWE'S WAS IN A TOUGH SPOT.

IT WAS THE SECOND LARGEST HOME IMPROVEMENT RETAILER IN THE WORLD, BUT WAS FACING SOME STUBBORN HEADWINDS.

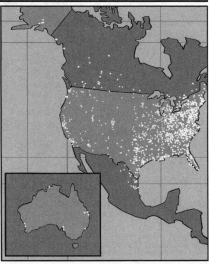

AFTER DECADES OF RAPID GROWTH, A QUICK GLANCE AT THE MAP MADE IT CLEAR THAT LOWE'S HAD SATURATED THE US MARKET.

SEARCHING FOR GROWTH, LOWE'S HAD EXPANDED INTO MEXICO, CANADA, AND AUSTRALIA.

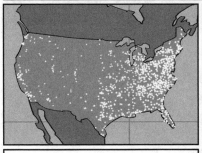

AS LOWE'S FACED UP TO THEIR FUTURE, THEY SEEMED CAUGHT IN THE SAME BIND AS SO MANY OTHER BIG COMPANIES.

BIG, PROFITABLE, RISK-AVERSE, AND TETHERED TO QUARTERLY EARNINGS.

THEIR OWN SUCCESS IN RETAIL MEANT THAT THEY DIDN'T HAVE THE NECESSARY DESIRE, CAPABILITIES, OR SUPPORT FROM SHAREHOLDERS TO DO SOMETHING TRANSFORMATIONAL.

THE FUTURE LOOKED UNCERTAIN.

BUT SIX YEARS LATER, LOWE'S FUTURE TURNED OUT TO BE VERY DIFFERENT.

LOWE'S SENT THE FIRST HARDWARE STORE IN SPACE.

THEY BUILT THE FIRST 3D PRINT AND SCAN SERVICES IN STORES...

...EVEN ATTRACTING CUSTOMERS FROM NEIGHBORING STATES.

THEY INTRODUCED SOME OF THE FIRST RETAIL ROBOTS IN ACTUAL USE, TAKING INVENTORY AT NIGHT AND GREETING CUSTOMERS.

THEY INTRODUCED EMPLOYEE EXO-SUITS -- SOFT ROBOTIC SKELETONS THAT HELP WORKERS CARRY HEAVY ITEMS -- THAT HAVE GENERATED INTEREST AROUND THE WORLD.

EVEN FURTHER, LOWE'S SOLD AUGMENTED-REALITY SMARTPHONES -- NEXT GEN "DIGITAL POWER TOOLS," -- IN STORES.

REMEMBER HOW EVERYONE THOUGHT APPLE -- A COMPUTER COMPANY -- WAS CRAZY TO TRY AND SELL YOU A PHONE?

THESE AR PHONES FLEW OFF THE SHELVES.

EVERYONE UNDERSTOOD THAT IF WE DIDN'T BUILD IT, SOMEONE ELSE SURELY WOULD.

AFTER READING THE COMIC BOOK, OUR EXECUTIVE TEAM SAW MY VISION TOO, AND THEY SAID:

GO BUILD IT!

WE FOUNDED THE LOWE'S INNOVATION LABS TO HELP US QUICKLY BUILD WHAT WE SAW IN THE STORIES.

ROBOTS, VIRTUAL- AND AUGMENTED-REALITY SHOWROOMS, EXOSUITS, AND MORE.

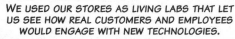

WE USED OUR STORES AS LIVING LABS THAT LET US SEE HOW REAL CUSTOMERS AND EMPLOYEES WOULD ENGAGE WITH NEW TECHNOLOGIES.

And here, Kyle has gotten to the second lesson of the process...

...breaking decision bottlenecks.

The retail robots didn't start in Lowe's, but in its subsidiary, Orchard Supply Hardware.

Why?

Kyle scrapped the org charts and mapped out how decisions were really made.

He approached his leadership team at Orchard about robots in stores, because they operated outside of the more rigid core.

They proved to be some of my earliest supporters!

Next, we built metrics for building the future, like applied neuroscience, that would help us understand and predict behavior.

I partnered with my PhD advisor, Dr. Thomas Ramsøy, to conduct neuroscience research that helped us make decisions based on data instead of instinct.

Planning for what they would adopt today, what they would adopt five years from now, and what they may never adopt.

THIS BECAME A REPEATABLE PROCESS THAT HELPED US GET FURTHER, FASTER THAN WE HAD EVER IMAGINED.

THROUGH THIS APPROACH, LOWE'S AND ITS PARTNERS GAINED THE INSIGHTS NEEDED TO MAKE EVIDENCE-BASED DECISIONS IN THE HIGHLY UNCERTAIN TERRAIN OF GROUNDBREAKING INNOVATION AND TRANS-FORMATION.

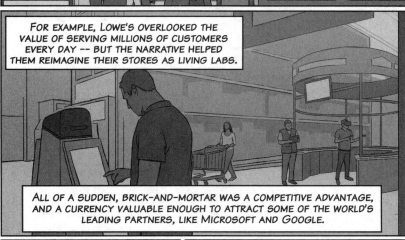

FOR EXAMPLE, LOWE'S OVERLOOKED THE VALUE OF SERVING MILLIONS OF CUSTOMERS EVERY DAY -- BUT THE NARRATIVE HELPED THEM REIMAGINE THEIR STORES AS LIVING LABS.

ALL OF A SUDDEN, BRICK-AND-MORTAR WAS A COMPETITIVE ADVANTAGE, AND A CURRENCY VALUABLE ENOUGH TO ATTRACT SOME OF THE WORLD'S LEADING PARTNERS, LIKE MICROSOFT AND GOOGLE.

NOW THERE ARE TOOLS TO HELP YOU NAVIGATE THROUGH THE UKNOWN. TOOLS THAT PROVIDE EVIDENCE-BASED SIGNPOSTS TO GUIDE YOUR DECISIONS.

SO REMEMBER, START WITH A NARRATIVE TO IDENTIFY THE END GOAL, THEN WORK BACKWARDS TO BRING IT TO LIFE, TESTING AND ITERATING ALL ALONG THE WAY.

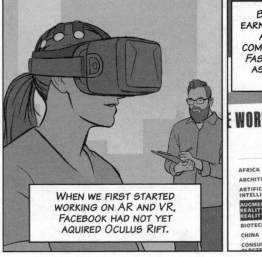

ACKNOWLEDGMENTS

We would like to acknowledge all those who contributed their time and thoughts toward this book. We would like to thank Melinda Merino for her thoughtful editorial advice and encouragement. We would also like to extend a special thank you and acknowledgment to Amanda Manna for her tireless work editing chapters, correcting drafts, and contributing stories. We would also like to thank all the leaders interviewed in this book, especially those who allowed us to speak openly about their successes and failures.

In addition, Nathan would like to express his deep gratitude to his family—Susannah Adore, Jordan Elisabeth, George van Waters, Josephine Apollo, and Beatrix Cosi—for their patience while he wrote the book. He would also like to thank his colleagues at INSEAD for their support, particularly Peter Zemsky and Andrew Shipilov, as well as his research assistants Devon Scott and Logan Bailey.

Kyle would like to thank his wonderful wife, Almira, and his daughter Alice.

Thomas would like to thank his wife, Majken, and his children, Sophia Lilje, Frederik, and Mike.

Chapter 1

1. Phalguni Soni, "Which International Opportunities Is Lowe's Betting On?" Market Realist, January 27, 2016, https://marketrealist.com /2016/01/lowes-takes-strategic-view-international-businesses; Jonathan Levin and Cristiane Luchesi, "Lowe's Said to Seek Acquisitions in Brazil," *The Charlotte Observer*, August 18, 2014, http://www.charlotteobserver.com /news/business/article9152720.html#.U_SmrPldXE0; Hollie Shaw, "Retail Giants Walmart, Sears, and Lowe's Are Suffering in Canada, *Financial Post*, October 6, 2014, http://business.financialpost.com/news/retail -marketing/retail-giants-such-as-walmart-sears-and-lowes-are-suffering-in -canada; Andria Cheng, "Lowe's Changes Lack Direction: Analyst," *MarketWatch*, January 7, 2013, https://www.marketwatch.com/story /lowes-changes-lack-direction-analyst-2013-01-07.

2. Megan Lewis, "Mission Accomplished: Houston, We Have 3D Printing," *Lowe's Open House*, August 24, 2016, https://newsroom.lowes .com/fresh-thinking/lowes-3d-printer-brings-tools-to-space/; Valerie Williams, "Innovation to Help Customers," *Lowe's Open House*, June 15, 2017, https://newsroom.lowes.com/fresh-thinking/lowes-innovates-to-help -customers/.

3. "Lowe's Introduces LoweBot—The Next Generation Robot to Enhance the Home Improvement Shopping Experience in the Bay Area," August 30, 2016, press release, https://newsroom.lowes.com/news-releases /lowesintroduceslowebot-thenextgenerationrobottoenhancethehomeimprov ementshoppingexperienceinthebayarea-2/.

4. Kristen Owen, "New Suit, Empowering Employees," *Lowe's Open House*, May 15, 2017, https://newsroom.lowes.com/fresh-thinking/new-suit -empowering-employees/.

5. "Lowe's Delivers Augmented Reality, Now Available on Aisle 3," press release, November 3, 2016, https://newsroom.lowes.com/news-releases/low esdeliversaugmentedrealitynowavailableonaisle3/.

6. Jeremy Kaplan, "Lowe's Prints Comic Books Imagining Sci-Fi Futures—Then Makes Them Real," *Digital Trends*, September 6, 2017, https://www.digitaltrends.com/virtual-reality/lowes-innovation-lab -comics/.

7. Matt McFarland, "These Lowe's Employees Are Now Wearing Exoskeletons to Work," *CNNTech*, May 15, 2017, http://money.cnn.com /2017/05/15/technology/lowes-exosuit/index.html.

8. Kaplan, "Lowe's Prints Comic Books Imagining Sci-Fi Futures—Then Makes Them Real."

9. Michael Thompson, "How Lowe's CEO Went from Corner Store to Corner Office," *Lowe's Open House*, September 5, 2016, https:// newsroom.lowes.com/inside-lowes/how-lowes-ceo-went-from-corner-store -to-corner-office/.

10. "Kyle Nel (Lowe's): What We Really Think of AR: A Behavioral Scientist's View," Augmented World Expo, June 5, 2017, https://www .youtube.com/watch?v=5QKxcABlHSI.

11. Masahiro Mori, "The Uncanny Valley," *Energy* 7.4 (1970): 33–35; Jun'ichiro Seyama and Ruth S. Nagayama, "The Uncanny Valley: Effect of Realism on the Impression of Artificial Human Faces," *Presence: Teleoperators and Virtual Environments* 16.4 (2007): 337–351; H. Brenton, M. Gillies, D. Ballin, and D. Chatting, "The Uncanny Valley: Does It Exist," 19th British HCI Group Annual Conference; "Kyle Nel (Lowe's): What We Really Think of AR: A Behavioral Scientist's View."

12. "Lowe's Purpose: To Help People Love Where They Live," https:// www.loweslink.com/llmain/pubdocuments/Lowes_Vision_Statement.pdf.

13. For an example of what Kyle's AR and VR demonstration looked like, see Kyle Nel, "How Science Fiction Is Shaping the Future of Retailing," TEDx Talk, February 28, 2015, https://www.youtube.com/watch?v=k8tg -eL8Y68.

14. Jon Russell, "Pokémon Go Has Now Crossed $1 Billion in Revenue," *TechCrunch*, February 1, 2017, https://techcrunch.com/2017/02/01/report -pokemon-go-has-now-crossed-1-billion-in-revenue/; https://newzoo.com /insights/articles/analysis-pokemon-go.

15. Michael E. Porter and James E. Heppelmann, "Why Every Organization Needs an Augmented Reality Strategy," *Harvard Business Review*, November–December 2017.

16. https://www.lowes.com/pd/Lenovo-Phab-2-Pro-6-4-in-64-GB-16 -MP-Smartphone-with-Tango-Technology/1000172295.

17. "Lowe's Purpose."

18. Tali Sharot, *The Influential Mind: What the Brain Reveals about Our Power to Change Others* (New York: Henry Holt and Company, 2017).

19. Aaron De Smet, Gerald Lackey, and Leigh M. Weiss, "Untangling Your Organization's Decision Making," *McKinsey Quarterly*, June 2017, www.mckinsey.com/business-functions/organization/our-insights /untangling-your-organizations-decision-making.

20. Voltaire, *Philosophical Dictionary*, selected and trans. H. I. Woolf (Mineola, NY: Dover Publications, 2010).

21. Gianfranco Zaccai, "Why Focus Groups Kill Innovation," *Co.Design*, October 18, 2012, www.fastcodesign.com/1671033/why-focus -groups-kill-innovation-from-the-designer-behind-swiffer.

22. Kyle Nel, "Why Attention, Emotion, and Cognition Are the Currency of the Future," *LinkedIn*, July 11, 2017, https://www .linkedin.com/pulse/why-attention-emotion-cognition-currency-future -kyle-nel/.

Chapter 2

1. The experiment was eventually published as a book chapter in 1990. See Charles N. Alexander and Ellen J. Langer, *Higher Stages of Human Development: Perspectives on Adult Growth* (New York: Oxford University Press, 1990). It was then retold in Ellen J. Langer, *Counterclockwise: Mindful Health and the Power of Possibility* (New York: Random House Digital, 2009).

2. Alia J. Crum and Ellen J. Langer, "Mind-Set Matters: Exercise and the Placebo Effect," *Psychological Science* 18, vol. 2 (2007): 165–171.

3. Langer, *Counterclockwise*; K. Feinberg, "The Mindfulness Chronicles," *Harvard Magazine*, September–October 2010.

4. Chanmo Park et al., "Blood Sugar Level Follows Perceived Time Rather Than Actual Time in People with Type 2 Diabetes," *Proceedings of the National Academy of Sciences* 113, vol. 29 (2016): 8168–8170.

5. Daniel Kahneman, *Thinking, Fast and Slow* (New York: Macmillan, 2011); Scott Plous, *The Psychology of Judgment and Decision Making* (New York: McGraw-Hill, 1993).

6. Dorothy Leonard, "The Limitations of Listening," *Harvard Business Review*, January 2002, 93.

7. Elizabeth F. Loftus and James M. Doyle, *Eyewitness Testimony: Civil and Criminal* (Charlottesville, VA: Michie Co., 1992).

8. Emily Kerry, "Could Woolly Mammoths Walk Again?," *Science in the News* (blog), Graduate School of Arts and Sciences, Harvard University, March 18, 2017, http://sitn.hms.harvard.edu/flash/2017/woolly -mammoths-walk.

9. Richard Malsbarger, "Seeding the Future of Helping People Love Where They Live." LinkedIn, September 19, 2017, https://www.linkedin .com/pulse/seeding-future-helping-people-love-where-live-richard -maltsbarger/?lipi=urn%3Ali%3Apage%3Ad_flagship3_profile_view_base %3B58TbQ3xOR2%2BcacCkcvfRjg%3D%3D.

10. Jeremy Kaplan, "Lowe's Prints Comic Books Imagining Sci-Fi Futures—Then Makes Them Real," *Digital Trends*, September 6, 2017, https://www.digitaltrends.com/virtual-reality/lowes-innovation-lab-comics/.

11. Alfred Sonnenfeld, Cesar Biojo, Kyle Nel, Mathieu Carenzo, Mikel Amo, and Paco Gimena, "The Unexpected Way," TEDx Universidad de Navarra, February 28, 2015, https://www.ted.com/tedx/events/14038.

12. "8 Groundbreaking Inventions Inspired by Science Fiction," *Quirky*, February 14, 2017, https://shop.quirky.com/blogs/news /inventions-inspired-by-science-fiction.

13. Phil Libin, interview with author (Nathan Furr), July 2017; Mike Brown, "Amazon CEO Jeff Bezos Says 'Star Trek' Inspired Alexa and Echo," *Inverse*, May 18, 2016, www.inverse.com/article/15865-amazon -ceo-jeff-bezos-says-star-trek-inspired-alexa-and-echo; Neil Strauss, "Elon Musk: The Architect of Tomorrow," *Rolling Stone*, November 15, 2017, www.rollingstone.com/culture/features/elon-musk-inventors-plans-for -outer-space-cars-finding-love-w511747.

14. Libin, interview with author.

15. Brian David Johnson, *Science Fiction Prototyping: Designing the Future with Science Fiction* (San Rafael, CA: Morgan & Claypool, 2011).

16. As quoted in Maria Popova, "Ursula K. Le Guin on Power, Oppression, Freedom, and How Imaginative Storytelling Expands Our Scope of the Possible," *Brain Pickings* (blog), May 6, 2016, www.brainpickings.org /2016/05/06/ursula-k-le-guin-freedom-oppression-storytelling.

17. Libin, interview with author.

18. Corinne Ruff, "Why Lowe's Uses Comic Books to Guide Innovation," RetailDive, October 5, 2017, https://www.retaildive.com/news /why-lowes-uses-comic-books-to-guide-innovation/506504/.

19. Paula Rogo, "MC Lyte Hosts Socially Conscious Hip-Hop Competition 'Pitch & Flow,'" *Essence,* September 16, 2017, https://www .essence.com/culture/mc-lyte-pitch-flow-hiphop-competition.

20. Maria Popova, "Neil Gaiman on How Stories Last," *Brain Pickings* (blog), June 16, 2015, www.brainpickings.org/2015/06/16/neil-gaiman -how-stories-last.

21. Uri Hasson et al., "Intersubject Synchronization of Cortical Activity during Natural Vision," *Science* 303.5664 (March 12, 2004): 1634–1640; Tali Sharot, *The Influential Mind: What the Brain Reveals about Our Power to Change Others* (New York: Henry Holt and Company, 2017).

22. Ibid.

23. Greg J. Stephens, Lauren J. Silbert, and Uri Hasson, "Speaker–Listener Neural Coupling Underlies Successful Communication," *Proceedings of the National Academy of Sciences* 107, no. 32 (2010): 14,425–14,430.

24. Jacek P. Dmochowski et al., "Audience Preferences Are Predicted by Temporal Reliability of Neural Processing," *Nature Communications* 5 (2014): 4567.

25. Megan French and Jeff Hancock, "What's the Folk Theory? Reasoning about Cyber-Social Systems" (February 2, 2017), available at SSRN: https://ssrn.com/abstract=2910571; Susan A. Gelman and Cristine H. Legare, "Concepts and Folk Theories," *Annual Review of Anthropology* 40 (2011): 379–398.

26. Jeff Hancock, interview with author (Nathan Furr), September 2017.

27. Shmuel "Mooly" Eden, interview with author (Nathan Furr), September 2017.

28. "Friday Poem: 'Elegy for David Beynon,' Leslie Norris," *Seren Books* (blog), October 21, 2016, https://serenbooks.wordpress.com/2016/10/21/friday-poem-elegy-for-david-beynon-leslie-norris.

29. Raghu Garud, Henri A. Schildt, and Theresa K. Lant, "Entrepreneurial Storytelling, Future Expectations, and the Paradox of Legitimacy," *Organization Science* 25, no. 5 (2014): 1479–1492.

30. Richy Rosario, "MC Lyte Hosts 'Pitch & Flow,' A Hip-Hop Competition for Socially Conscious Initiatives," *Vibe*, September 14, 2017, www.vibe.com/2017/09/mc-lyte-pitch-flow-competition-socially-conscious-initiatives.; XXL Staff, "MC Lyte to Host Pitch & Flow Event at John F. Kennedy Family Theater in Washington, D.C.," *XXL*, September 12, 2017, http://www.xxlmag.com/news/2017/09/mc-lyte-pitch-and-flow/.

31. Nira Liberman and Yaacov Trope, "The Role of Feasibility and Desirability Considerations in Near and Distant Future Decisions: A Test of Temporal Construal Theory," *Journal of Personality and Social Psychology* 75, no. 1 (1998): 5; Yaacov Trope and Nira Liberman, "Temporal Construal," *Psychological Review* 110, no. 3 (2003): 403; Garud, Schildt, and Lant, "Entrepreneurial Storytelling."

32. Garud, Schildt, and Lant, "Entrepreneurial Storytelling."

33. P. Hansen, "Networks, Narratives, and New Markets: The Rise and Decline of Danish Modern Furniture Design, 1930–1970," *Business History Review* 80 (2006): 449–483.

34. Spencer H. Harrison and Samir Nurmohamed, "Hearing Crickets? An Inductive Study of Overcoming Negative Reactions to Radical Creativity," working paper, INSEAD, Fontainebleau, France, 2018.

35. Harrison and Nurmohamed, "Hearing Crickets?"; Spencer Harrison and Samir Nurmohamed, "Does It Bug You?," working paper, INSEAD, Fontainebleau, France, 2018.

36. Andrew Hargadon and Robert I. Sutton, "Technology Brokering and Innovation in a Product Development Firm," *Administrative Science Quarterly* 42, no. 4 (1997): 716–749.

Chapter 3

1. As reported in Charles Duhigg, *The Power of Habit: Why We Do What We Do and How to Change* (New York: Random House, 2013), 97–101.

2. Ibid.

3. M. S. Christensen et al., "An fMRI Study of the Neural Correlates of Graded Visual Perception," *NeuroImage* 31, no. 4 (2006): 1711–1725; M. Overgaard et al., "Is Conscious Perception Gradual or Dichotomous? A Comparison of Report Methodologies during a Visual Task," *Consciousness and Cognition* 15, no. 4 (2006): 700–708; Thomas Z. Ramsøy and Martin Skov, "Brand Preference Affects the Threshold for Perceptual Awareness," *Journal of Consumer Behaviour* 13, no. 1 (2014): 1–8; Thomas Z. Ramsøy and Morten Overgaard, "Introspection and Subliminal Perception," *Phenomenology and the Cognitive Sciences* 3 (2004): 1–23.

4. B. J. Baars, S. Franklin, and Thomas Z. Ramsøy, "Global Workspace Dynamics: Cortical 'Binding and Propagation' Enables Conscious Contents," *Frontiers in Psychology* 4 (2013): 200; B. J. Baars, Thomas Z. Ramsøy, and S. Laureys, "Brain, Conscious Experience and the Observing Self," *Trends in Neurosciences* 26, no. 12 (2003): 671–675.

5. Daniel Kahneman, "A Perspective on Judgment and Choice: Mapping Bounded Rationality," *American Psychologist* 58, no. 9 (2003): 697; Keith E. Stanovich and Richard F. West, "Individual Differences in Reasoning: Implications for the Rationality Debate?," *Behavioral and Brain Sciences* 23, no. 5 (2000): 645–665; Daniel Kahneman, *Thinking, Fast and Slow* (New York: Macmillan, 2011).

6. Kahneman, "A Perspective on Judgment and Choice"; Ellen J. Langer, Arthur Blank, and Benzion Chanowitz, "The Mindlessness of Ostensibly Thoughtful Action: The Role of 'Placebic' Information in Interpersonal Interaction," *Journal of Personality and Social Psychology* 36, no. 6 (1978): 635.

7. Daniel Kahneman, "Maps of Bounded Rationality: Psychology for Behavioral Economics," *American Economic Review* 93, no. 5 (2003): 1449–1475.

8. Mark Goodman, interview with author (Kyle Nel), October 2017.

9. Jeffrey Pfeffer, *Managing with Power: Politics and Influence in Organizations* (Boston: Harvard Business Press, 1992).

10. Thomas Allen and Gunter Henn, *The Organization and Architecture of Innovation* (New York: Routledge, 2007).

11. Thomas Z. Ramsøy and Martin Skov, "How Genes Make Up Your Mind: Individual Biological Differences and Value-Based Decisions," *Journal of Economic Psychology* 31, no. 5 (2010): 818–831.

12. Joseph Campbell, *The Hero with a Thousand Faces*, vol. 17 (Novato, CA: New World Library, 2008); Joseph Campbell and Bill Moyers, *The Power of Myth* (New York: Anchor, 2011); Carl Gustav Jung, *The Archetypes and the Collective Unconscious* (New York: Routledge, 2014); Duane P. Schultz and Sydney Ellen Schultz, *A History of Modern Psychology* (Australia; United States: Cengage Learning, 2015).

13. Ramsøy and Skov, "How Genes Make Up Your Mind."

14. Thomas Z. Ramsøy et al., "Empathy as a Neuropsychological Heuristic in Social Decision-Making," *Social Neuroscience* 10, no. 2 (2015): 179–191; Julian Macoveanu et al., "The Neural Bases of Framing Effects in Social Dilemmas," *Journal of Neuroscience, Psychology, and Economics* 9, no. 1 (2016): 14.

15. Ramsøy et al., "Empathy as a Neuropsychological Heuristic in Social Decision-Making."

16. Morten Friis-Olivarius et al., "Imaging the Creative Unconscious: Reflexive Neural Responses to Objects in the Visual and Parahippocampal Region Predicts State and Trait Creativity," *Scientific Reports* 7, no. 1 (2017): 14,420.

17. Dan Ariely, *Predictably Irrational: The Hidden Forces That Shape Our Decisions*, Rev. and expanded ed. (New York: Harper Perennial, 2010).

18. Paul H. Thibodeau and Lera Boroditsky, "Metaphors We Think With: The Role of Metaphor in Reasoning," PLOS ONE 6, no. 2 (2011): e16782.

Chapter 4

1. Ming Hsu et al., "Neural Systems Responding to Degrees of Uncertainty in Human Decision-Making," *Science* 310, no. 5754 (2005): 1680–1683.

2. Ibid.

3. Caroline J. Charpentier et al., "Enhanced Risk Aversion, But Not Loss Aversion, in Unmedicated Pathological Anxiety," *Biological Psychiatry* 81, no. 12 (2017): 1014–1022; Mithu Storoni, "The Real Reason Your Brain Is So Scared of Failure," *Inc.*, accessed April 30, 2018, www.inc.com/mithu -storoni/your-brain-isnt-afraid-of-failure-heres-whats-really-going-on.html.

4. Kyle Nel, "Why Attention, Emotion, and Cognition Are the Currency of the Future," *LinkedIn*, July 11, 2017, https://www.linkedin.com /pulse/why-attention-emotion-cognition-currency-future-kyle-nel/.

5. "Lowe's Canada Introduces Lowe's Holoroom for Immersive Design Experience," press release, November 21, 2014, https://newsroom.lowes .com/news-releases/lowes-canada-introduces-lowes-holoroom-immersive -design-experience/.

6. Author presentation (Kyle Nel) at 2017 Google I/O conference (https://www.youtube.com/watch?v=BOrg2oc3-rQ); also verified in re-search for clients unrelated to Lowe's research.

7. Andrew Gelman, "'Any Old Map Will Do' Meets 'God Is in Every Leaf of Every Tree,'" *Statistical Modeling, Causal Inference, and Social Science* (blog), April 23, 2012, http://andrewgelman.com/2012/04/23/any -old-map-will-do-meets-god-is-in-every-leaf-of-every-tree.

8. Because many people have made this statement or a variant of it, we cannot attribute it precisely. Nonetheless, we acknowledge that we are not the first to say this comment, and we are paraphrasing from many giants who have gone before us.

9. Raghu Garud, Henri A. Schildt, and Theresa K. Lant, "Entrepre-neurial Storytelling, Future Expectations, and the Paradox of Legitimacy," *Organization Science* 25, no. 5 (2014): 1479–1492.

10. Nick Bilton, *Hatching Twitter: A True Story of Money, Power, Friendship, and Betrayal* (New York: Penguin, 2014).

11. Garud, Schildt, and Lant, "Entrepreneurial Storytelling, Future Ex-pectations, and the Paradox of Legitimacy."

12. Ellen O'Connor, "Storied Business: Typology, Intertextuality, and Traffic in Entrepreneurial Narrative," *Journal of Business Communication* 39, no. 1 (2002): 36–54; Liliana Doganova and Marie Eyquem-Renault, "What Do Business Models Do? Innovation Devices in Technology Entre-preneurship," *Research Policy* 38, no. 10 (2009): 1559–1570; Garud, Schildt, and Lant, "Entrepreneurial Storytelling, Future Expectations, and the Par-adox of Legitimacy."

13. G. S. Berns and S. E. Moore, "A Neural Predictor of Cultural Pop-ularity," *Journal of Consumer Psychology: The Official Journal of the Society for Consumer Psychology* 22, no. 1 (2012): 154–160.

14. M. A. S. Boksem and A. Smidts, "Brain Responses to Movie-Trailers Predict Individual Preferences for Movies and Their Population-Wide Com-mercial Success," *Journal of Marketing Research* 52, no. 4 (2014): 482–492.

15. B. Knutson et al., "Neural Predictors of Purchases," *Neuron* 53, no. 1 (2007): 147–156.

16. J. P. Dmochowski et al., "Audience Preferences Are Predicted by Temporal Reliability of Neural Processing," *Nature Communications* 5 (2014): 1–9.

17. S. J. Smith, B. T. Stone, T. Ranatunga, K. Nel, T. Z. Ramsøy, and C. Berka, "Neurophysiological Indices of Human Social Interactions Between Humans and Robots," in C. Stephanidis (ed.), *Communications in Computer and Information Science*, vol. 713 (2017), https://link.springer.com /chapter/10.1007/978-3-319-58750-9_36.

18. A. G. Greenwald, D. E. McGhee, and J. L. K. Schwartz, "Measuring Individual Differences in Implicit Cognition: The Implicit Association Test," *Journal of Personality and Social Psychology* 74, no. 6 (1998): 1464– 1480, http://faculty.fortlewis.edu/burke_b/Senior/BLINK%20replication /IAT.pdf; W. Hofmann, B. Gawronski, T. Gschwendner, H. Le, and M. Schmitt, "A Meta-Analysis on the Correlation Between the Implicit Association Test and Explicit Self-Report Measures," *Personality and Social Psychology Bulletin* (2003), https://psydok.psycharchives.de/jspui /bitstream/20.500.11780/64/1/beri158.pdf; D. Maison, A. G. Greenwald, and R. H. Bruin, "Predictive Validity of the Implicit Association Test in Studies of Brands, Consumer Attitudes, and Behavior," *Journal of Consumer Psychology* 14 (no. 4): 405–415, http://faculty.washington.edu/agg/pdf /Maison&al.JCP.2004.pdf; and A. G. Greenwald, E. L. Uhlmann, T. A. Poehlman, and Mahzarin R. Banaji, "Understanding and Using the Implicit Association Test: III. Meta-Analysis of Predictive Validity," *Journal of Personality and Social Psychology* 97, no. 1 (2009): 17–41, http://faculty .washington.edu/agg/pdf/GPU&B.meta-analysis.JPSP.2009.pdf.

Chapter 5

1. Christopher Bonanos, "Steve Jobs and Edwin Land," *Polaroid Land*, January 20, 2012, www.polaroidland.net/2012/01/20/steve-jobs-and -edwin-land; Christopher Bonanos, "The Man Who Inspired Jobs," *New York Times*, October 7, 2011, www.nytimes.com/2011/10/07/opinion/the -man-who-inspired-jobs.html?pagewanted=all.

2. Bonanos, "The Man Who Inspired Jobs"; "Why Steve Jobs Said Meeting the Founder of Polaroid Was 'Like Visiting a Shrine,'" *The Economist*, March 29, 2015, www.businessinsider.com/why-steve-jobs -said-meeting-the-founder-of-polaroid-was-like-visiting-a-shrine-2015-3 ?IR=T.

3. Nathan McAlone, "This Man Invented the Digital Camera in 1975—And His Bosses at Kodak Never Let It See the Light of Day," *Business Insider*, August 17, 2015, www.businessinsider.com/this-man-invented -the-digital-camera-in-1975-and-his-bosses-at-kodak-never-let-it-see-the -light-of-day-2015-8?IR=T.

4. M. Tripsas and G. Gavetti, "Capabilities, Cognition and Inertia: Evidence from Digital Imaging," *Strategic Management Journal* 21 (2000): 1147–1161.

5. Ralph Leighton, *Surely You're Joking, Mr. Feynman!: Adventures of a Curious Character* (London: Vintage, 1992).

6. *Wikipedia*, s.v. "negative capability," last modified December 28, 2017, https://en.wikipedia.org/wiki/Negative_capability; Maria Popova, "The Art of 'Negative Capability': Keats on Embracing Uncertainty and Celebrating the Mysterious," *Brain Pickings* (blog), November 1, 2012, www.brainpickings.org/2012/11/01/john-keats-on-negative-capability.

7. Popova, "The Art of 'Negative Capability'"; *Wikipedia*, s.v. "negative capability."

8. *Wikipedia*, s.v. "Kaospilot," last modified March 8, 2017, https://en.wikipedia.org/wiki/Kaospilot; Kaospilot, "We Can Look Very Serious, But Really: We Are a Playground," Kaospilot Switzerland web page, accessed April 30, 2018, www.kaospilots.ch/school; Dorte Hygum Sørensen, "Business School for KaosPilots," *Fast Company*, June 30, 1996, www.fastcompany.com/27098/business-school-kaospilots; Kaospilot, "Kaospilot in Brief," company web page, accessed April 30, 2018, www.kaospilot.dk/about/story.

9. Christer Windeløv-Lidzélius and David Storkholm, "KaosPilot Creative Leadership: Christer Windeløv-Lidzélius and David Storkholm at TEDxRVA 2013," video, *YouTube*, posted July 1, 2013, www.youtube.com/watch?v=K4U8a6eYyEY.

10. Jeremy Kaplan, "Lowe's Prints Comic Books Imagining Sci-Fi Futures—Then Makes Them Real," *Digital Trends*, September 6, 2017, https://www.digitaltrends.com/virtual-reality/lowes-innovation-lab-comics/.

11. Lowe's Innovation Labs, "Made in Space," Lowe's Innovation Labs web page, accessed April 30, 2018, www.lowesinnovationlabs.com/madeinspace.

12. Nathan Furr and Andrew Shipilov, "Building the Right Ecosystem for Innovation," *Sloan Management Review*, Summer 2018; Nathan Furr, Kate O'Keeffe, and Jeffrey H. Dyer, "Managing Multiparty Innovation," *Harvard Business Review*, November 2016, 76–83.

13. Furr and Shipilov, "Building the Right Ecosystem for Innovation."

14. Alex Knapp, "Made In Space Is Successfully Taking Manufacturing into the Stars," *Forbes*, August 31, 2017, www.forbes.com/sites/alexknapp/2017/08/31/made-in-space-is-successfully-taking-manufacturing-into-the-stars/#25c430187d8d; Made In Space, "Made In Space: Archinaut," Made In Space web page, accessed April 30, 2018, http://madeinspace.us/archinaut.

15. Kristin Owen, "New Suit, Empowering Employees," *Lowe's Open House*, May 15, 2017, https://newsroom.lowes.com/fresh-thinking/new-suit-empowering-employees/.

16. Nathan Furr, Kate O'Keeffe, and Jeffrey H. Dyer, "Managing Multiparty Innovation," *Harvard Business Review*, November 2016, 76–83.

17. Ibid.

18. For Intuit's framework, see Nathan Furr and Jeffrey H. Dyer, *The Innovator's Method: Bringing the Lean Startup into Your Organization* (Boston: Harvard Business Review Press, 2014), 62.

19. Everett M. Rogers, *Diffusion of Innovations* (New York: Simon and Schuster, 2010); Barbara Wejnert, "Integrating Models of Diffusion of Innovations: A Conceptual Framework," *Annual Review of Sociology* 28 (August 2002): 297–326.

20. Maria Popova, "Friedrich Nietzsche on Why a Fulfilling Life Requires Embracing Rather than Running from Difficulty," *Brain Pickings* (blog), October 15, 2014, www.brainpickings.org/2014/10/15/nietzsche-on-difficulty.

21. Ibid.

22. Maria Popova, "A Noble New Year's Resolution from Nietzsche," *Brain Pickings* (blog), January 2, 2015, www.brainpickings.org/2015/01/02/nietzsche-new-year-resolution.

Epilogue

1. Gordon J. Pearson, *Rise and Fall of Management: A Brief History of Practice, Theory, and Context* (Burlington, VT: Gower, 2012).

2. Nathan Furr and Jeffrey H. Dyer, *The Innovator's Method: Bringing the Lean Startup into Your Organization* (Boston: Harvard Business Review Press, 2014), 20.

3. Donna Kelly, Slavica Singer, and Mike Herrington, "2015/2016 Global Entrepreneurship Monitor," Global Entrepreneurship Monitor, 2017, http://www.gemconsortium.org.

4. Scott D. Anthony et al., "2018 Corporate Longevity Forecast: Creative Destruction Is Accelerating," Innosight, February 2018, www.innosight.com/insight/creative-destruction/.

5. Furr and Dyer, *The Innovator's Method*.

6. Derived from Nathan Furr, J. A. Nickerson, and R. Wuebker, "A Theory of Entrepreneuring," working paper, INSEAD, Fontainbleau, France, 2016.

7. Furr and Dyer, *The Innovator's Method*.

8. Q. N. Huy, "Emotional Balancing of Organizational Continuity and Radical Change: The Contribution of Middle Managers," *Administrative Science Quarterly* 47, no. 1 (2002): 31; Q. N. Huy, K. G. Corley, and M. S. Kraatz, "From Support to Mutiny: Shifting Legitimacy Judgments and Emotional Reactions Impacting the Implementation of Radical Change," *Academy of Management Journal* 57, no. 6 (2014): 1650–1680.

9. M. J. Benner and M. Tripsas, "The Influence of Prior Industry Affiliation on Framing in Nascent Industries: The Evolution of Digital Cameras," *Strategic Management Journal* 33, no. 3 (2012): 277–302; D. A. Grégoire, P. S. Barr, and D. A. Shepherd, "Cognitive Processes of Opportunity Recognition: The Role of Structural Alignment," *Organization Science* 21, no. 2 (2010): 413–431; Daniel Kahneman, *Thinking, Fast and Slow* (New York: Macmillan, 2011).

10. Morten Friis-Olivarius et al., "Imaging the Creative Unconscious: Reflexive Neural Responses to Objects in the Visual and Parahippocampal Region Predicts State and Trait Creativity," *Scientific Reports* 7, no. 1 (2017): 14,420.

11. P. S. Barr, "Adapting to Unfamiliar Environmental Events: A Look at the Evolution of Interpretation and Its Role in Strategic Change," *Organization Science* 9 (1998): 644–669; P. S. Barr, J. L. Stimpert, and A. S. Huff, "Cognitive Change, Strategic Action, and Organizational Renewal," *Strategic Management Journal* 13 (1992): 15–36; J. P. Eggers and S. Kaplan, "Cognition and Renewal: Comparing CEO and Organizational Effects on Incumbent Adaptation to Technical Change," *Organization Science* 20, no. 2 (2009): 461–477; S. Kaplan, "Cognition, Capabilities, and Incentives: Assessing Firm Response to the Fiber-Optic Revolution," *Academy of Management Journal* 51, no. 4 (2008): 672–695; B. M. Staw, L. E. Sandelands, and J. E. Dutton, "Threat-Rigidity Effects in Organizational Behavior: A Multi-Level Analysis," *Administrative Science Quarterly* 26, no. 4 (1981): 501–524.

12. Jacek P. Dmochowski, "Audience Preferences Are Predicted by Temporal Reliability of Neural Processing," *Nature Communications* 5 (2014): 4567; Gregory S. Berns and Sara E. Moore, "A Neural Predictor Of Cultural Popularity," *Journal of Consumer Psychology* 22, no. 1 (2012): 154–160; A. Smidts et al., "Advancing Consumer Neuroscience," *Marketing Letters* 25, no. 3 (2014): 257–267; Spencer H. Harrison and Samir Nurmohamed, "Hearing Crickets? An Inductive Study of Overcoming Negative Reactions to Radical Creativity," working paper, INSEAD, Fontainebleau, France, 2018; Spencer Harrison et al., "Does It Bug You?," working paper, INSEAD, Fontainebleau, France, 2018.

Appendix A

1. David Whyte, "Song for the Salmon," in *The Three Marriages: Reimagining Work, Self, and Relationship* (New York: Riverhead Books, 2009).

2. Ibid.

3. Ben Feringa, in-person interview with author (Nathan Furr), Brussels, Belgium, October 2016.

Appendix B

1. Donna Kelly, Slavica Singer, and Mike Herrington, "2015/2016 Global Entrepreneurship Monitor," Global Entrepreneurship Monitor, 2017, http://www.gemconsortium.org.

2. Nathan Furr and Jeffrey H. Dyer, *The Innovator's Method: Bringing the Lean Startup into Your Organization* (Boston: Harvard Business Review Press, 2014).

3. Rajshree Agarwal and Michael Gort, "First-Mover Advantage and the Speed of Competitive Entry, 1887–1986," *Journal of Law and Economics* 44, no. 1 (2001): 161–177.

4. World Economic Forum, "Chapter 1: The Future of Jobs and Skills," in *The Future of Jobs*, by Till Alexander Leopold, Vesselina Ratcheva, and Saadia Zahidi, World Economic Forum, January 2016, http://reports.weforum.org/future-of-jobs-2016/chapter-1-the-future-of-jobs-and-skills.

5. Joseph Campbell, *The Hero with a Thousand Faces: The Collected Works of Joseph Campbell* (Novato, CA: New World Library, 2008).

Behavioral Economics, Psychology, and Social Psychology

Ariely, Dan. *Predictably Irrational: The Hidden Forces That Shape Our Decisions*. New York: HarperCollins, 2009.

Kahenman, Daniel. *Thinking, Fast and Slow*. New York: Penguin, 2012.

Plous, Scott. *The Psychology of Judgment and Decision Making*. Philadelphia: Temple University Press, 1993.

Ross, Lee, and Richard Nisbett. *The Person and the Situation: Perspectives of Social Psychology*. London: Pinter and Martin, 2011.

Thaler, Richard H., and Cass R. Sunstein. *Nudge: Improving Decisions about Health, Wealth, and Happiness*. New York: Penguin, 2009.

———. *Misbehaving: The Making of Behavioral Economics*. New York: W.W. Norton & Company, 2016.

Applied and Foundational Neuroscience

Churchland, Patricia S. *Neurophilosophy: Toward a Unified Science of the Mind-Brain*. Cambridge, MA: MIT Press, 1989.

Damasio, Antonio. *Descartes' Error: Emotion, Reason, and the Human Brain*. New York: Penguin, 2005.

Dehaene, Stanislas. *Consciousness and the Brain: Deciphering How the Brain Codes Our Thoughts*. New York: Penguin, 2014.

Gazzaniga, Michael S., Richard B. Ivry, and George R. Mangun. *Cognitive Neuroscience: The Biology of the Mind*. 4th ed. New York: W.W. Norton & Company, 2013.

Kandel, Eric R., ed. *Principles of Neural Science*. 5th ed. New York: McGraw-Hill Education/Medical, 2012.

LeDoux, Joseph. *The Emotional Brain: The Mysterious Underpinnings of Emotional Life*. New York: Simon & Schuster, 1998.

Innovation

Brown, Tim. *Change by Design: How Design Thinking Transforms Organizations and Inspires Innovation*. New York: HarperBusiness, 2009.

Christensen, Clayton M. *The Innovator's Dilemma: When New Technologies Cause Great Firms to Fail*. Boston: Harvard Business Review Press, 2016.

Dyer, Jeffrey H., Hal Gregersen, and Clayton M. Christensen. *The Innovator's DNA: Mastering the Five Skills of Disruptive Innovators*. Boston: Harvard Business Review Press, 2011.

Furr, Nathan, and Jeffrey H. Dyer. *The Innovator's Method: Bringing the Lean Startup into Your Organization*. Boston: Harvard Business Review Press, 2014.

Osterwalder, Alexander, and Yves Pigneur. *Business Model Generation: A Handbook for Visionaries, Game Changers, and Challengers*. Hoboken, NJ: Wiley, 2010.

Ries, Eric. *The Lean Startup: How Today's Entrepreneurs Use Continuous Innovation to Create Radically Successful Businesses*. New York: Currency, 2011.

Sutherland, Jeff, and J. J. Sutherland. *Scrum: The Art of Doing Twice the Work in Half the Time*. New York: Currency, 2014.

Transformation

Anthony, Scott D., Clark G. Gilbert, and Mark W. Johnson. *Dual Transformation: How to Reposition Today's Business While Creating the Future*. Boston: Harvard Business Review Press, 2017.

Kotter, John P. *Leading Change, with a New Preface by the Author*. Boston: Harvard Business Review Press, 2012.

ABOUT THE AUTHORS

NATHAN FURR is a professor of strategy and innovation at INSEAD in Paris and a recognized expert in the fields of innovation and technology strategy. Professor Furr earned his PhD from the Stanford Technology Ventures Program at Stanford University, where he studied how innovators commercialize their ideas. He has published books and articles on the questions of how established companies innovate, how they respond to disruption, and how they can transform. His recent bestselling book, *The Innovator's Method* (Harvard Business Review Press, September 2014) won multiple awards from the business press. His previous book, *Nail It Then Scale It: The Entrepreneur's Guide to Creating and Managing Breakthrough Innovation* (June 2011), was one of the first and most successful books in the Lean Startup movement. He has also published over a dozen articles in top academic journals and practitioner outlets, such as *Harvard Business Review* and *Sloan Management Review*.

Professor Furr has worked with leading companies from across industries—including Google, Amazon, Citi, Intuit, Tesla, Philips, Kimberly-Clark, Telenor, Solvay, and others—to study and implement innovation strategies. Professor Furr also cofounded the International Business Model Competition, which attracts more than 2,500 teams from more than 250 universities around the world, and the Innovator's DNA, an organization devoted to building innovation capabilities in established companies.

KYLE NEL is the CEO and cofounder of Uncommon Partners, a transformation company. He previously founded Lowe's Innovation Labs (LIL), the disruptive innovation hub for the *Fortune* 40 home improvement company, and served as its Executive Director. In that role he created and led a team responsible for driving the company's innovation vision, strategy, and growth. Under his leadership, Lowe's Innovation Labs built a proprietary 3-D content creation and asset management platform; augmented and virtual reality stores; virtual reality DIY skills clinics; the first autonomous retail service robots; soft robotic exosuits capable of delivering lift assistance to store employees; and 3-D scanning and printing services at retail—and in space, where the first commercially manufactured object off the planet was a Lowe's wrench that was modified for astronauts. He also built a disruptive technology lab and incubator in Bangalore, India.

Nel sits on the boards of emerging tech companies and is a faculty member focused on corporate innovation at Singularity University in California. He is also a former member of the XPRIZE Foundation Innovation Board. He was recognized on the 2015 Advertising Age "40 under 40" list, and he received the 2016 "People Shaping Retail's Future" award from the National Retail Federation. He was also a founding member of the Retail Industry Leaders Association's (R)Tech Advisory Council. He previously held positions in market research with Lowe's and with the Walmart Global Insights Group. He holds an MBA from the A. C. Nielsen Center for Marketing Research at the University of Wisconsin and a bachelor's degree in business management from Brigham Young University–Idaho.

THOMAS ZOËGA RAMSØY is considered one of the leading figures in the field of applied neuroscience and is the author of many often-cited papers on the subject. He is driven by a curiosity to understand human behaviors, such as creativity, choice, and consumer adoption, and to create tools capable of both measuring and affecting such behaviors. Ramsøy founded Neurons Inc in 2013, and the company has seen exponential growth with offices now spread across four continents. As CEO at Neurons Inc, Ramsøy consults with leading global businesses and government agencies on employing neuroscience to improve business outcomes and achieve transformational success.

He previously founded the Center for Decision Neuroscience at the Copenhagen Business School and Copenhagen University Hospital, which has produced results shared in leading scientific journals. Ramsøy is acting editor and on the editorial board of multiple prominent scientific journals, such as *Frontiers in Neuroscience* and *Scientific Reports* (a *Nature* journal). He is a faculty member at Singularity University at the NASA Ames Research Center, and he teaches MBA courses at the Copenhagen Business School. Ramsøy has a master's degree and certification in neuropsychology, and he holds a PhD in neurobiology and neuroimaging.